Mometrix TEST PREPARATION

NCETMB

Secrets Study Guide

DEAR FUTURE EXAM SUCCESS STORY

First of all, **THANK YOU** for purchasing Mometrix study materials!

Second, congratulations! You are one of the few determined test-takers who are committed to doing whatever it takes to excel on your exam. **You have come to the right place.** We developed these study materials with one goal in mind: to deliver you the information you need in a format that's concise and easy to use.

In addition to optimizing your guide for the content of the test, we've outlined our recommended steps for breaking down the preparation process into small, attainable goals so you can make sure you stay on track.

We've also analyzed the entire test-taking process, identifying the most common pitfalls and showing how you can overcome them and be ready for any curveball the test throws you.

Standardized testing is one of the biggest obstacles on your road to success, which only increases the importance of doing well in the high-pressure, high-stakes environment of test day. Your results on this test could have a significant impact on your future, and this guide provides the information and practical advice to help you achieve your full potential on test day.

Your success is our success

We would love to hear from you! If you would like to share the story of your exam success or if you have any questions or comments in regard to our products, please contact us at **800-673-8175** or **support@mometrix.com**.

Thanks again for your business and we wish you continued success!

Sincerely,
The Mometrix Test Preparation Team

Need more help? Check out our flashcards at:
http://MometrixFlashcards.com/NCBTMB

Written and edited by the Mometrix Exam Secrets Test Prep Team
Printed in the United States of America

TABLE OF CONTENTS

Introduction

Thank you for purchasing this resource! You have made the choice to prepare yourself for a test that could have a huge impact on your future, and this guide is designed to help you be fully ready for test day. Obviously, it's important to have a solid understanding of the test material, but you also need to be prepared for the unique environment and stressors of the test, so that you can perform to the best of your abilities.

For this purpose, the first section that appears in this guide is the **Secret Keys**. We've devoted countless hours to meticulously researching what works and what doesn't, and we've boiled down our findings to the five most impactful steps you can take to improve your performance on the test. We start at the beginning with study planning and move through the preparation process, all the way to the testing strategies that will help you get the most out of what you know when you're finally sitting in front of the test.

We recommend that you start preparing for your test as far in advance as possible. However, if you've bought this guide as a last-minute study resource and only have a few days before your test, we recommend that you skip over the first two Secret Keys since they address a long-term study plan.

If you struggle with **test anxiety**, we strongly encourage you to check out our recommendations for how you can overcome it. Test anxiety is a formidable foe, but it can be beaten, and we want to make sure you have the tools you need to defeat it.

Secret Key #1 – Plan Big, Study Small

There's a lot riding on your performance. If you want to ace this test, you're going to need to keep your skills sharp and the material fresh in your mind. You need a plan that lets you review everything you need to know while still fitting in your schedule. We'll break this strategy down into three categories.

Information Organization

Start with the information you already have: the official test outline. From this, you can make a complete list of all the concepts you need to cover before the test. Organize these concepts into groups that can be studied together, and create a list of any related vocabulary you need to learn so you can brush up on any difficult terms. You'll want to keep this vocabulary list handy once you actually start studying since you may need to add to it along the way.

Time Management

Once you have your set of study concepts, decide how to spread them out over the time you have left before the test. Break your study plan into small, clear goals so you have a manageable task for each day and know exactly what you're doing. Then just focus on one small step at a time. When you manage your time this way, you don't need to spend hours at a time studying. Studying a small block of content for a short period each day helps you retain information better and avoid stressing over how much you have left to do. You can relax knowing that you have a plan to cover everything in time. In order for this strategy to be effective though, you have to start studying early and stick to your schedule. Avoid the exhaustion and futility that comes from last-minute cramming!

Study Environment

The environment you study in has a big impact on your learning. Studying in a coffee shop, while probably more enjoyable, is not likely to be as fruitful as studying in a quiet room. It's important to keep distractions to a minimum. You're only planning to study for a short block of time, so make the most of it. Don't pause to check your phone or get up to find a snack. It's also important to **avoid multitasking**. Research has consistently shown that multitasking will make your studying dramatically less effective. Your study area should also be comfortable and well-lit so you don't have the distraction of straining your eyes or sitting on an uncomfortable chair.

The time of day you study is also important. You want to be rested and alert. Don't wait until just before bedtime. Study when you'll be most likely to comprehend and remember. Even better, if you know what time of day your test will be, set that time aside for study. That way your brain will be used to working on that subject at that specific time and you'll have a better chance of recalling information.

Finally, it can be helpful to team up with others who are studying for the same test. Your actual studying should be done in as isolated an environment as possible, but the work of organizing the information and setting up the study plan can be divided up. In between study sessions, you can discuss with your teammates the concepts that you're all studying and quiz each other on the details. Just be sure that your teammates are as serious about the test as you are. If you find that your study time is being replaced with social time, you might need to find a new team.

Secret Key #2 – Make Your Studying Count

You're devoting a lot of time and effort to preparing for this test, so you want to be absolutely certain it will pay off. This means doing more than just reading the content and hoping you can remember it on test day. It's important to make every minute of study count. There are two main areas you can focus on to make your studying count.

Retention

It doesn't matter how much time you study if you can't remember the material. You need to make sure you are retaining the concepts. To check your retention of the information you're learning, try recalling it at later times with minimal prompting. Try carrying around flashcards and glance at one or two from time to time or ask a friend who's also studying for the test to quiz you.

To enhance your retention, look for ways to put the information into practice so that you can apply it rather than simply recalling it. If you're using the information in practical ways, it will be much easier to remember. Similarly, it helps to solidify a concept in your mind if you're not only reading it to yourself but also explaining it to someone else. Ask a friend to let you teach them about a concept you're a little shaky on (or speak aloud to an imaginary audience if necessary). As you try to summarize, define, give examples, and answer your friend's questions, you'll understand the concepts better and they will stay with you longer. Finally, step back for a big picture view and ask yourself how each piece of information fits with the whole subject. When you link the different concepts together and see them working together as a whole, it's easier to remember the individual components.

Finally, practice showing your work on any multi-step problems, even if you're just studying. Writing out each step you take to solve a problem will help solidify the process in your mind, and you'll be more likely to remember it during the test.

Modality

Modality simply refers to the means or method by which you study. Choosing a study modality that fits your own individual learning style is crucial. No two people learn best in exactly the same way, so it's important to know your strengths and use them to your advantage.

For example, if you learn best by visualization, focus on visualizing a concept in your mind and draw an image or a diagram. Try color-coding your notes, illustrating them, or creating symbols that will trigger your mind to recall a learned concept. If you learn best by hearing or discussing information, find a study partner who learns the same way or read aloud to yourself. Think about how to put the information in your own words. Imagine that you are giving a lecture on the topic and record yourself so you can listen to it later.

For any learning style, flashcards can be helpful. Organize the information so you can take advantage of spare moments to review. Underline key words or phrases. Use different colors for different categories. Mnemonic devices (such as creating a short list in which every item starts with the same letter) can also help with retention. Find what works best for you and use it to store the information in your mind most effectively and easily.

Secret Key #3 – Practice the Right Way

Your success on test day depends not only on how many hours you put into preparing, but also on whether you prepared the right way. It's good to check along the way to see if your studying is paying off. One of the most effective ways to do this is by taking practice tests to evaluate your progress. Practice tests are useful because they show exactly where you need to improve. Every time you take a practice test, pay special attention to these three groups of questions:

- The questions you got wrong
- The questions you had to guess on, even if you guessed right
- The questions you found difficult or slow to work through

This will show you exactly what your weak areas are, and where you need to devote more study time. Ask yourself why each of these questions gave you trouble. Was it because you didn't understand the material? Was it because you didn't remember the vocabulary? Do you need more repetitions on this type of question to build speed and confidence? Dig into those questions and figure out how you can strengthen your weak areas as you go back to review the material.

Additionally, many practice tests have a section explaining the answer choices. It can be tempting to read the explanation and think that you now have a good understanding of the concept. However, an explanation likely only covers part of the question's broader context. Even if the explanation makes perfect sense, **go back and investigate** every concept related to the question until you're positive you have a thorough understanding.

As you go along, keep in mind that the practice test is just that: practice. Memorizing these questions and answers will not be very helpful on the actual test because it is unlikely to have any of the same exact questions. If you only know the right answers to the sample questions, you won't be prepared for the real thing. **Study the concepts** until you understand them fully, and then you'll be able to answer any question that shows up on the test.

It's important to wait on the practice tests until you're ready. If you take a test on your first day of study, you may be overwhelmed by the amount of material covered and how much you need to learn. Work up to it gradually.

On test day, you'll need to be prepared for answering questions, managing your time, and using the test-taking strategies you've learned. It's a lot to balance, like a mental marathon that will have a big impact on your future. Like training for a marathon, you'll need to start slowly and work your way up. When test day arrives, you'll be ready.

Start with the strategies you've read in the first two Secret Keys—plan your course and study in the way that works best for you. If you have time, consider using multiple study resources to get different approaches to the same concepts. It can be helpful to see difficult concepts from more than one angle. Then find a good source for practice tests. Many times, the test website will suggest potential study resources or provide sample tests.

Practice Test Strategy

If you're able to find at least three practice tests, we recommend this strategy:

UNTIMED AND OPEN-BOOK PRACTICE

Take the first test with no time constraints and with your notes and study guide handy. Take your time and focus on applying the strategies you've learned.

TIMED AND OPEN-BOOK PRACTICE

Take the second practice test open-book as well, but set a timer and practice pacing yourself to finish in time.

TIMED AND CLOSED-BOOK PRACTICE

Take any other practice tests as if it were test day. Set a timer and put away your study materials. Sit at a table or desk in a quiet room, imagine yourself at the testing center, and answer questions as quickly and accurately as possible.

Keep repeating timed and closed-book tests on a regular basis until you run out of practice tests or it's time for the actual test. Your mind will be ready for the schedule and stress of test day, and you'll be able to focus on recalling the material you've learned.

Secret Key #4 – Pace Yourself

Once you're fully prepared for the material on the test, your biggest challenge on test day will be managing your time. Just knowing that the clock is ticking can make you panic even if you have plenty of time left. Work on pacing yourself so you can build confidence against the time constraints of the exam. Pacing is a difficult skill to master, especially in a high-pressure environment, so **practice is vital**.

Set time expectations for your pace based on how much time is available. For example, if a section has 60 questions and the time limit is 30 minutes, you know you have to average 30 seconds or less per question in order to answer them all. Although 30 seconds is the hard limit, set 25 seconds per question as your goal, so you reserve extra time to spend on harder questions. When you budget extra time for the harder questions, you no longer have any reason to stress when those questions take longer to answer.

Don't let this time expectation distract you from working through the test at a calm, steady pace, but keep it in mind so you don't spend too much time on any one question. Recognize that taking extra time on one question you don't understand may keep you from answering two that you do understand later in the test. If your time limit for a question is up and you're still not sure of the answer, mark it and move on, and come back to it later if the time and the test format allow. If the testing format doesn't allow you to return to earlier questions, just make an educated guess; then put it out of your mind and move on.

On the easier questions, be careful not to rush. It may seem wise to hurry through them so you have more time for the challenging ones, but it's not worth missing one if you know the concept and just didn't take the time to read the question fully. Work efficiently but make sure you understand the question and have looked at all of the answer choices, since more than one may seem right at first.

Even if you're paying attention to the time, you may find yourself a little behind at some point. You should speed up to get back on track, but do so wisely. Don't panic; just take a few seconds less on each question until you're caught up. Don't guess without thinking, but do look through the answer choices and eliminate any you know are wrong. If you can get down to two choices, it is often worthwhile to guess from those. Once you've chosen an answer, move on and don't dwell on any that you skipped or had to hurry through. If a question was taking too long, chances are it was one of the harder ones, so you weren't as likely to get it right anyway.

On the other hand, if you find yourself getting ahead of schedule, it may be beneficial to slow down a little. The more quickly you work, the more likely you are to make a careless mistake that will affect your score. You've budgeted time for each question, so don't be afraid to spend that time. Practice an efficient but careful pace to get the most out of the time you have.

Secret Key #5 – Have a Plan for Guessing

When you're taking the test, you may find yourself stuck on a question. Some of the answer choices seem better than others, but you don't see the one answer choice that is obviously correct. What do you do?

The scenario described above is very common, yet most test takers have not effectively prepared for it. Developing and practicing a plan for guessing may be one of the single most effective uses of your time as you get ready for the exam.

In developing your plan for guessing, there are three questions to address:

- When should you start the guessing process?
- How should you narrow down the choices?
- Which answer should you choose?

When to Start the Guessing Process

Unless your plan for guessing is to select C every time (which, despite its merits, is not what we recommend), you need to leave yourself enough time to apply your answer elimination strategies. Since you have a limited amount of time for each question, that means that if you're going to give yourself the best shot at guessing correctly, you have to decide quickly whether or not you will guess.

Of course, the best-case scenario is that you don't have to guess at all, so first, see if you can answer the question based on your knowledge of the subject and basic reasoning skills. Focus on the key words in the question and try to jog your memory of related topics. Give yourself a chance to bring the knowledge to mind, but once you realize that you don't have (or you can't access) the knowledge you need to answer the question, it's time to start the guessing process.

It's almost always better to start the guessing process too early than too late. It only takes a few seconds to remember something and answer the question from knowledge. Carefully eliminating wrong answer choices takes longer. Plus, going through the process of eliminating answer choices can actually help jog your memory.

Summary: Start the guessing process as soon as you decide that you can't answer the question based on your knowledge.

How to Narrow Down the Choices

The next chapter in this book (**Test-Taking Strategies**) includes a wide range of strategies for how to approach questions and how to look for answer choices to eliminate. You will definitely want to read those carefully, practice them, and figure out which ones work best for you. Here though, we're going to address a mindset rather than a particular strategy.

Your odds of guessing an answer correctly depend on how many options you are choosing from.

Number of options left	5	4	3	2	1
Odds of guessing correctly	20%	25%	33%	50%	100%

You can see from this chart just how valuable it is to be able to eliminate incorrect answers and make an educated guess, but there are two things that many test takers do that cause them to miss out on the benefits of guessing:

- Accidentally eliminating the correct answer
- Selecting an answer based on an impression

We'll look at the first one here, and the second one in the next section.

To avoid accidentally eliminating the correct answer, we recommend a thought exercise called **the $5 challenge**. In this challenge, you only eliminate an answer choice from contention if you are willing to bet $5 on it being wrong. Why $5? Five dollars is a small but not insignificant amount of money. It's an amount you could afford to lose but wouldn't want to throw away. And while losing $5 once might not hurt too much, doing it twenty times will set you back $100. In the same way, each small decision you make—eliminating a choice here, guessing on a question there—won't by itself impact your score very much, but when you put them all together, they can make a big difference. By holding each answer choice elimination decision to a higher standard, you can reduce the risk of accidentally eliminating the correct answer.

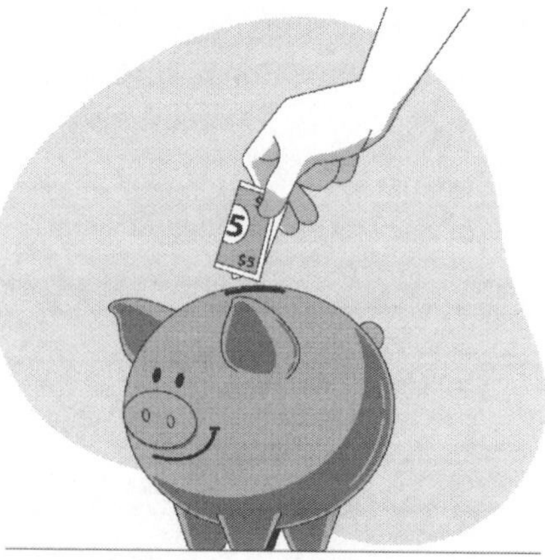

The $5 challenge can also be applied in a positive sense: If you are willing to bet $5 that an answer choice *is* correct, go ahead and mark it as correct.

Summary: Only eliminate an answer choice if you are willing to bet $5 that it is wrong.

Which Answer to Choose

You're taking the test. You've run into a hard question and decided you'll have to guess. You've eliminated all the answer choices you're willing to bet $5 on. Now you have to pick an answer. Why do we even need to talk about this? Why can't you just pick whichever one you feel like when the time comes?

The answer to these questions is that if you don't come into the test with a plan, you'll rely on your impression to select an answer choice, and if you do that, you risk falling into a trap. The test writers know that everyone who takes their test will be guessing on some of the questions, so they intentionally write wrong answer choices to seem plausible. You still have to pick an answer though, and if the wrong answer choices are designed to look right, how can you ever be sure that you're not falling for their trap? The best solution we've found to this dilemma is to take the decision out of your hands entirely. Here is the process we recommend:

Once you've eliminated any choices that you are confident (willing to bet $5) are wrong, select the first remaining choice as your answer.

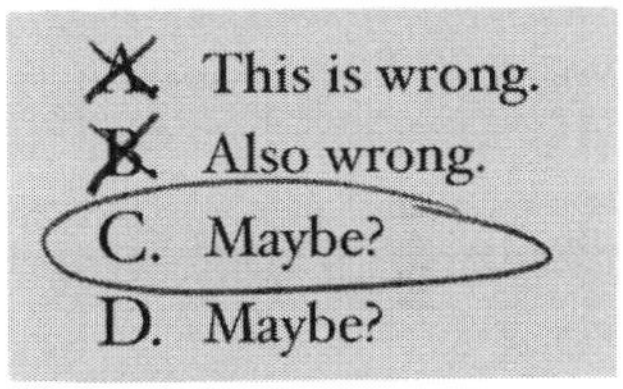

Whether you choose to select the first remaining choice, the second, or the last, the important thing is that you use some preselected standard. Using this approach guarantees that you will not be enticed into selecting an answer choice that looks right, because you are not basing your decision on how the answer choices look.

This is not meant to make you question your knowledge. Instead, it is to help you recognize the difference between your knowledge and your impressions. There's a huge difference between thinking an answer is right because of what you know, and thinking an answer is right because it looks or sounds like it should be right.

Summary: To ensure that your selection is appropriately random, make a predetermined selection from among all answer choices you have not eliminated.

Test-Taking Strategies

This section contains a list of test-taking strategies that you may find helpful as you work through the test. By taking what you know and applying logical thought, you can maximize your chances of answering any question correctly!

It is very important to realize that every question is different and every person is different: no single strategy will work on every question, and no single strategy will work for every person. That's why we've included all of them here, so you can try them out and determine which ones work best for different types of questions and which ones work best for you.

Question Strategies

✓ Read Carefully

Read the question and the answer choices carefully. Don't miss the question because you misread the terms. You have plenty of time to read each question thoroughly and make sure you understand what is being asked. Yet a happy medium must be attained, so don't waste too much time. You must read carefully and efficiently.

✓ Contextual Clues

Look for contextual clues. If the question includes a word you are not familiar with, look at the immediate context for some indication of what the word might mean. Contextual clues can often give you all the information you need to decipher the meaning of an unfamiliar word. Even if you can't determine the meaning, you may be able to narrow down the possibilities enough to make a solid guess at the answer to the question.

✓ Prefixes

If you're having trouble with a word in the question or answer choices, try dissecting it. Take advantage of every clue that the word might include. Prefixes can be a huge help. Usually, they allow you to determine a basic meaning. *Pre-* means before, *post-* means after, *pro-* is positive, *de-* is negative. From prefixes, you can get an idea of the general meaning of the word and try to put it into context.

✓ Hedge Words

Watch out for critical hedge words, such as *likely, may, can, often, almost, mostly, usually, generally, rarely*, and *sometimes*. Question writers insert these hedge phrases to cover every possibility. Often an answer choice will be wrong simply because it leaves no room for exception. Be on guard for answer choices that have definitive words such as *exactly* and *always*.

✓ Switchback Words

Stay alert for *switchbacks*. These are the words and phrases frequently used to alert you to shifts in thought. The most common switchback words are *but, although*, and *however*. Others include *nevertheless, on the other hand, even though, while, in spite of, despite*, and *regardless of*. Switchback words are important to catch because they can change the direction of the question or an answer choice.

⊘ FACE VALUE

When in doubt, use common sense. Accept the situation in the problem at face value. Don't read too much into it. These problems will not require you to make wild assumptions. If you have to go beyond creativity and warp time or space in order to have an answer choice fit the question, then you should move on and consider the other answer choices. These are normal problems rooted in reality. The applicable relationship or explanation may not be readily apparent, but it is there for you to figure out. Use your common sense to interpret anything that isn't clear.

Answer Choice Strategies

⊘ ANSWER SELECTION

The most thorough way to pick an answer choice is to identify and eliminate wrong answers until only one is left, then confirm it is the correct answer. Sometimes an answer choice may immediately seem right, but be careful. The test writers will usually put more than one reasonable answer choice on each question, so take a second to read all of them and make sure that the other choices are not equally obvious. As long as you have time left, it is better to read every answer choice than to pick the first one that looks right without checking the others.

⊘ ANSWER CHOICE FAMILIES

An answer choice family consists of two (in rare cases, three) answer choices that are very similar in construction and cannot all be true at the same time. If you see two answer choices that are direct opposites or parallels, one of them is usually the correct answer. For instance, if one answer choice says that quantity x increases and another either says that quantity x decreases (opposite) or says that quantity y increases (parallel), then those answer choices would fall into the same family. An answer choice that doesn't match the construction of the answer choice family is more likely to be incorrect. Most questions will not have answer choice families, but when they do appear, you should be prepared to recognize them.

⊘ ELIMINATE ANSWERS

Eliminate answer choices as soon as you realize they are wrong, but make sure you consider all possibilities. If you are eliminating answer choices and realize that the last one you are left with is also wrong, don't panic. Start over and consider each choice again. There may be something you missed the first time that you will realize on the second pass.

⊘ AVOID FACT TRAPS

Don't be distracted by an answer choice that is factually true but doesn't answer the question. You are looking for the choice that answers the question. Stay focused on what the question is asking for so you don't accidentally pick an answer that is true but incorrect. Always go back to the question and make sure the answer choice you've selected actually answers the question and is not merely a true statement.

⊘ EXTREME STATEMENTS

In general, you should avoid answers that put forth extreme actions as standard practice or proclaim controversial ideas as established fact. An answer choice that states the "process should be used in certain situations, if..." is much more likely to be correct than one that states the "process should be discontinued completely." The first is a calm rational statement and doesn't even make a definitive, uncompromising stance, using a hedge word *if* to provide wiggle room, whereas the second choice is far more extreme.

✓ Benchmark

As you read through the answer choices and you come across one that seems to answer the question well, mentally select that answer choice. This is not your final answer, but it's the one that will help you evaluate the other answer choices. The one that you selected is your benchmark or standard for judging each of the other answer choices. Every other answer choice must be compared to your benchmark. That choice is correct until proven otherwise by another answer choice beating it. If you find a better answer, then that one becomes your new benchmark. Once you've decided that no other choice answers the question as well as your benchmark, you have your final answer.

✓ Predict the Answer

Before you even start looking at the answer choices, it is often best to try to predict the answer. When you come up with the answer on your own, it is easier to avoid distractions and traps because you will know exactly what to look for. The right answer choice is unlikely to be word-for-word what you came up with, but it should be a close match. Even if you are confident that you have the right answer, you should still take the time to read each option before moving on.

General Strategies

✓ Tough Questions

If you are stumped on a problem or it appears too hard or too difficult, don't waste time. Move on! Remember though, if you can quickly check for obviously incorrect answer choices, your chances of guessing correctly are greatly improved. Before you completely give up, at least try to knock out a couple of possible answers. Eliminate what you can and then guess at the remaining answer choices before moving on.

✓ Check Your Work

Since you will probably not know every term listed and the answer to every question, it is important that you get credit for the ones that you do know. Don't miss any questions through careless mistakes. If at all possible, try to take a second to look back over your answer selection and make sure you've selected the correct answer choice and haven't made a costly careless mistake (such as marking an answer choice that you didn't mean to mark). This quick double check should more than pay for itself in caught mistakes for the time it costs.

✓ Pace Yourself

It's easy to be overwhelmed when you're looking at a page full of questions; your mind is confused and full of random thoughts, and the clock is ticking down faster than you would like. Calm down and maintain the pace that you have set for yourself. Especially as you get down to the last few minutes of the test, don't let the small numbers on the clock make you panic. As long as you are on track by monitoring your pace, you are guaranteed to have time for each question.

✓ Don't Rush

It is very easy to make errors when you are in a hurry. Maintaining a fast pace in answering questions is pointless if it makes you miss questions that you would have gotten right otherwise. Test writers like to include distracting information and wrong answers that seem right. Taking a little extra time to avoid careless mistakes can make all the difference in your test score. Find a pace that allows you to be confident in the answers that you select.

⊘ Keep Moving

Panicking will not help you pass the test, so do your best to stay calm and keep moving. Taking deep breaths and going through the answer elimination steps you practiced can help to break through a stress barrier and keep your pace.

Final Notes

The combination of a solid foundation of content knowledge and the confidence that comes from practicing your plan for applying that knowledge is the key to maximizing your performance on test day. As your foundation of content knowledge is built up and strengthened, you'll find that the strategies included in this chapter become more and more effective in helping you quickly sift through the distractions and traps of the test to isolate the correct answer.

Now that you're preparing to move forward into the test content chapters of this book, be sure to keep your goal in mind. As you read, think about how you will be able to apply this information on the test. If you've already seen sample questions for the test and you have an idea of the question format and style, try to come up with questions of your own that you can answer based on what you're reading. This will give you valuable practice applying your knowledge in the same ways you can expect to on test day.

Good luck and good studying!

General Knowledge of Body Systems

Skeletal System

The skeletal system is made up of about 206 bones and the cartilage and ligaments that hold them together. The exact number of bones may vary slightly from person to person. The axial portion of the skeleton includes the skull, hyoid bone, spinal column and rib cage, while the appendicular portion consists of the pelvis, arms and legs. Bones are organs made of living tissue, but they are fairly rigid structures. Their rigidity comes from the calcified material and collagen that give them their form. Bone tissue also contains bone cells, blood vessels, and other minerals besides calcium, connective tissues and marrow. Marrow is the source of red blood cell production. Bones have a hard outer layer called compact bone and a softer inner layer. The ends of the bones are also made primarily of this softer tissue, which is called spongy bone.

Muscular System

The organs of the muscular system are muscles, the tissue is specialized to contract and relax to produce movement. There are three types of muscle tissue: skeletal, cardiac and visceral. Muscle tissue is voluntary if it is under conscious control, and involuntary if it is controlled automatically by the brain. Muscle tissue is further classified as striated or smooth, according to its visible structure. Skeletal muscle is striated and voluntary. Cardiac muscle, found only in the heart, is striated and involuntary. Visceral muscle, which occurs in the linings of organs and blood vessels, is smooth and involuntary. Cardiac muscle cells have a distinguishing feature, called the intercalated disc, a section at the end of the cell where it meets another.

Nervous System

The nervous system is the central control for the body. Its functions include the monitoring of changes in the internal and external environments; organization, analysis and storage of information; and action based on the information. There are two anatomical parts of the nervous system: the central nervous system (CNS) and the peripheral nervous system (PNS). The components of the CNS are the brain and spinal cord. The PNS consists of the nerves that run throughout the body. The nervous system can be further divided into four aspects according to function: sensory, motor, somatic and autonomic systems. The sensory system relays information from the body's senses to the CNS. The motor system transfers impulses from the CNS to muscles, glands and other organs to promote action. Via the somatic system, a person consciously controls the skeletal muscles for purposeful action. Finally, the autonomic system operates organs and functions which one does not have conscious control, such as cardiac muscle and smooth muscle tissues.

Endocrine System

The endocrine system controls much of the body's physiology by means of secretions called hormones. Hormones are chemicals generated in one part of the body to produce a result in another. Hormones are transmitted through the blood stream and other body fluids. The primary organs of the endocrine system are the glands that produce these secretions: the pituitary, situated just under the brain; the thyroid in the neck; the parathyroid that are attached to the thyroid; the adrenals sitting on top of the kidneys; the pineal located in the brain; the pancreas, an abdominal organ; the thymus, situated in the chest between the lungs; and the reproductive glands which are the ovaries in women and the testes in men. During pregnancy the placenta also acts like an endocrine gland.

Heart

The heart is primarily muscle tissue and is located in the chest slightly left of center. Structurally it is four-chambered having two atria and two ventricles. Blood enters the right atrium and is pumped by the right ventricle through the pulmonary arteries where it picks up oxygen from the lungs. The blood then comes back to the heart, entering the left atrium, and is pumped by the left ventricle out into the circulatory system which carries it through the body. A system of one-way valves controls the flow of blood into and out of the heart and between the atria and the ventricles. Blood enters the heart by way of the vena cava, travels for oxygenation through the pulmonary artery, returns to the left side of the heart via the pulmonary vein, and travels out into the body through the aorta.

Lymphatic System

The lymphatic system is important to both the circulatory system and the body's immune functions. The lymphatic system collects interstitial fluid and returns it to the circulatory system via the veins. This fluid is called lymph during this process. The lymphatic system also filters the fluid and produces white blood cells called lymphocytes that destroy invading microorganisms as part of the immune system. Some important anatomical features of the lymphatic system, in addition to the lymph itself, are lymphatic capillaries and vessels and the lymph nodes. The lymphatic capillaries transport fluids from the tissues into the lymphatic system. The capillaries merge into lymphatic vessels to drain lymph from the larger anatomical regions. Lymph nodes are masses of lymphatic tissue that form white blood cells and are part of the immune system. The thymus, a glandular structure located in the chest, and the spleen are also part of the lymphatic system.

Process of Respiration

Oxygen is carried to the cells of the body by the respiratory and circulatory systems working together. Oxygen is taken to the cells, and carbon dioxide is carried away as a waste product. There are four stages in the process of respiration. First, pulmonary ventilation brings air into the lungs and expels air from them. During external respiration, blood in the lungs receives oxygen for transport throughout the body, and carbon dioxide is taken from the blood into the lungs for expulsion. Next, the cardiovascular system pumps the oxygenated blood through the body to nourish tissues and cells. Finally, the oxygenated blood passes into the tissues through the capillaries, and carbon dioxide is removed from the cells and tissues for transport back to the lungs.

Digestive System

The purpose of the digestive system is to break down food into components small enough to be absorbed into the bloodstream. The pathway food follows in the process from the mouth to the anus is called the alimentary canal. It consists of the mouth, pharynx, esophagus, stomach, and small and large intestines. Other organs participating in digestion are called accessory organs and include the teeth and salivary glands, liver, gallbladder and pancreas. Digestion is described as having two processes, mechanical and chemical digestion. During mechanical digestion, food is broken down into smaller components. During chemical digestion, food molecules are broken down further into smaller molecules that can be absorbed by the body.

Urinary System

The two main functions of the urinary system are waste elimination and fluid balance maintenance. In this latter capacity, it also plays a major role in electrolyte and pH balance. The four major components of the urinary system are the kidneys, ureters, urinary bladder and urethra. The kidneys are a pair of glands located in the back of the abdomen. They filter waste products out of the blood, help regulate electrolytes and produce urine for expulsion from the body. Urine is composed mainly of uric acid, water, ammonia and urea. Urine passes from the kidneys to the bladder via the ureters, which are tube-like structures made of muscle tissue. The urinary bladder stores the urine until it can be expelled. Urine is expelled from the body through the urethra, another tube-like structure.

Review Video: Urinary System
Visit mometrix.com/academy and enter code: 601053

Female Reproductive System

The female gonads are the ovaries, which produce ova or egg cells. The terms uterine tubes, fallopian tubes and oviducts are interchangeable and refer to the ducts that transport egg cells out of the ovaries. The uterus receives the ovum and provides the environment for a developing embryo if the ovum is fertilized. The vagina is an elastic tube-like passageway between the uterus and the outside, separated from the uterus by the cervix, which is really the end of the uterus. The female external genitalia are collectively called the vulva. The component parts of the vulva are the labia majora and labia minora (folds of skin around the vaginal opening), the vestibule (the space between the labia minora), and the clitoris (a small piece of erectile tissue just in front of the urethral opening). The vestibular glands, also called Bartholin's glands, are located on each side of the vaginal opening and secrete a lubricating fluid into the vestibule.

Male Reproductive System

The male gonads are the testes, or testicles, which function to produce spermatozoa, or sperm cells. On route to the outside, sperm cells are carried in fluid called semen and pass through a series of ducts which are the epididymis, vas deferens, ejaculatory duct and urethra. The secretions of several sets of glands facilitate the processes of the male reproductive system. The seminal vesicles secrete a substance that regulates the pH of semen and provides fructose as an energy source for sperm cells. The prostate also contributes to the pH of semen and stimulates sperm cell movement. The bulbourethral glands secrete fluid that neutralizes the pH in the urethra and lubricates the end of the penis. The male external genitalia are the scrotum, which contains the testes, and the penis.

Movement

Body mechanics applies physical laws of motion to biological systems, especially the human body and the way it moves. Also called biomechanics, this approach uses concepts of levers, fulcrums, and the application of force to understand how muscles and bones move the body and cause it to perform actions.

Kinesiology is the study of movement and uses biomechanical principles and anatomy to understand how the body moves and performs.

Applied kinesiology is a system of muscle testing in order to evaluate functional capacity. It views muscle function as a set of physical, mechanical processes.

Gait refers to how a person walks. Gait can reveal biomechanical problems related to structure and function of the body. A normal gait is smooth and rhythmic. A gait cycle includes a stance phase and a swing phase. During the stance phase the heel strikes the floor, the foot slaps down, there is a pause called the midstance, and then the heel lifts followed by the toes. During the swing phase there is first acceleration, when the foot is swinging from the back toward the midline, followed by midswing when the leg hangs at the midline. The third component is deceleration as the foot swings forward of the midline. Gait also includes the concurrent movements of the arms, called arm swing. Gait involves movements of the pelvis, hip, knee, ankle and foot. Neuromuscular and musculoskeletal problems are the most common causes of abnormal gait, but weight and issues with balance can influence gait also.

Meridians

In traditional Chinese medicine (TCM) theory the life force, Chi, travels through the body via a system of channels or meridians. At various points along the way, Chi comes up to the surface of the body, and these points are those used in acupuncture and acupressure treatments. There are 365 of these points. Chief among these channels are twelve primary meridians and two extraordinary meridians. The meridians are paired and associated with Yin or Yang forces. All begin or end in the feet and hands. Yin channels run along the front of the body and Yang channels along the back of the body. The primary meridians are named for organs of the body, but they are associated with much more than the organ for which they are named. The Yin primary meridians come together in the extraordinary meridian called Ren, and the Yang primary meridians in the extraordinary meridian Du.

Chakra System

According to traditional Indian medicine, the Chakras are seven energy centers arranged vertically from the base of the spine to the top of the head. They correspond generally to centers of nerve ganglia and nerve plexuses. In traditional Indian concepts of the body, the Chakras are represented as spinning discs associated with colors, elements, sounds, senses, physiological processes, and emotional states. Disease and emotional stress can upset the balance of energy in one or more Chakras and disrupt the flow of life energy through the body. Conversely, work with Chakras can be used to restore energy balance and flow, and the associated physical and emotional disturbances. Chakra work is done via body work, meditation, visualization, color therapy, aroma therapy and yoga among possible approaches.

Body Systems

The following systems of the body:

Cardiovascular (also called the circulatory system): Chief components are the heart, blood vessels, and blood components, which carry oxygen and other necessary ingredients to the body tissues and carry away waste products.

Digestive: Consists of the alimentary canal, from mouth to anus, and the supporting glands and organs. Breaks down food into useable nutrients and transfers the nutrients to the blood.

Endocrine: A system of glands and associated tissues that regulate physiological functions by secreting hormones.

Integumentary: Skin, hair, and associated glandular tissues. Encloses and protects the body, provides sense of touch, excretes waste through sweat, helps regulate body temperature.

Lymphatic: Consists of fluid and vessels, as well as lymph nodes and glandular tissues. Serves as part of the immune system and transfers material between the blood and organs.

Muscular: The skeletal muscles. Produces movement, generates body heat, and maintains body position and posture.

Nervous: The nerves, spinal cord, and brain. Communicates information across the body, regulates activity of endocrine glands, controls muscle movements.

Reproductive: Internal and external genitalia, ovaries and testes, and associated glands and organs. Produces ova in women and sperm in men, and performs functions of procreation.

Respiratory: Lungs and bronchial airways. Brings in oxygen and distributes it into the blood. Removes waste gasses from the blood for elimination.

Skeletal: Bones, cartilage, ligaments, and tendons. It is the body's frame supporting structure and movement. Bone marrow produces blood cells.

Urinary: Kidneys, bladder, urethra, and the connections between them. Stores waste for elimination and regulate salt/water balance.

Body Cavities

The body cavities describe regions of the body according to groupings of internal organs contained in those regions. There are nine body cavities:

Abdominal: Contains lower digestive organs including the stomach, small intestine, colon, liver and spleen.

Pelvic: Holds the urinary bladder, rectum and reproductive organs.

Abdominopelvic: Describes the abdominal and pelvic cavities combined.

Thoracic: The chest cavity inside the rib cage, containing the heart and lungs.

Pericardial: Contains the heart, within the thoracic cavity.

Cranial: Contains the brain.

Spinal: Encloses the spinal cord.

Ventral: The thoracic and abdominopelvic cavities combined.

Dorsal: The cranial and spinal cavities combined.

Directional Terms

The following directional terms as they are used in discussions of anatomy:

Anterior (or ventral): On or in the direction of the front of the body.

Caudal (or inferior): Below or toward the lower end of the body.

Cephalad: In the direction of the head.

Cranial (or superior): On or in the direction of the head.

Distal: Out from the trunk of the body.

Dorsal (posterior): On or toward the back side of the body.

Inferior (caudal): Lower down on the body.

Lateral: Out toward the sides, away from the body's midline.

Medial: Inwards, toward the body's midline.

Posterior (dorsal): In the direction of the back side of the body, or behind some point of reference.

Proximal: Back toward the trunk of the body.

Superficial: On or closer to the external surface of the body.

Superior (or cranial or cephalad): Upwards in the direction of the head.

Ventral (or anterior): On or in the direction of the front of the body.

Anatomy, Physiology, & Kinesiology

The Skeletal System

FUNCTIONS OF BONES

The five generally recognized functions of bones are as follows:

Support: Bones provide a frame for the rest of the body.

Movement: Muscles attach to the bones, which come together at articulated joints. This system makes it possible for the body to move about and to apply force necessary to carry out activities and functions.

Protection: Bones can act like shields for the more vulnerable organs of the body. For example, the brain is encased in the skull, and the rib cage surrounds the lungs and heart.

Mineral storage: Most of the body's calcium is stored in the bones. The body withdraws calcium from the skeleton as needed to maintain optimum levels of calcium in the blood.

Formation of blood cells: In a process called hemopoiesis, blood cells are formed in the marrow of the sternum, ribs, vertebrae, cranial bones, femur and humerus.

LONG BONES

Articular cartilage: Also called hyaline cartilage. This covers the broad ends of the long bones and provides a protective cushion against impact.

Diaphysis: The long, hollow portion of the long bone.

Endosteum: The membrane lining the hollow cavity of a long bone and containing bone cells called osteoblasts that are responsible for depositing calcium in the bones.

Epiphysis: The wide part at each end of a long bone. These are made up of softer tissue than the diaphysis, and provide places for muscles to attach. In immature bones epiphysial cartilage lies between the diaphysis and the epiphysis.

Medullary cavity: The hollow shaft inside the long bone. It contains the marrow.

Periosteum: A tissue covering the outside of the long bone, except at the ends. This tissue contains nerves and blood vessels, and also osteoblasts.

PERIOSTEUM

The periosteum is a membrane that covers the surface of bones. It is fundamentally a connective tissue. Because it is a tough, fibrous material it serves to protect the bone underneath it. It also contains blood vessels that transfer nourishment to the bone tissue, and osteoblasts that contribute to bone growth and maintenance by depositing calcium in the bone. Thus the periosteum is necessary to bone growth and repair. There are also nerves running through the periosteum, which make bone bruises very painful. It attaches to the underlying bone by means of fibers that penetrate the bone tissue and bond the two together. These fibers also interweave with tendon tissue to connect muscles to bones.

Skeletal Terms

Condyle: A rounded area usually on the end of a bone and often forming part of a joint.

Crest: A large ridge on a bone where muscles can attach.

Epicondyle: A further prominent area on a condyle for muscle attachment.

Facet: A flat, smooth area that forms part of a joint with another bone.

Fissure: A thin opening like a crack, but naturally occurring as part of the bone's anatomy making a place for blood vessels or nerves.

Foramen: A hole in the bone where blood vessels, nerves or connective tissues pass through.

Fossa: A depression in the bone sometimes as part of a joint.

Groove: A long, narrow depression in the bone where blood vessels or nerves can lie.

Head: The wine-colored portion on the ends of bones, usually serving as part of a joint.

Line: A small ridge on the bone where muscles attach.

Malleolus: A projection sticking out to either side of the end of a bone, on the end that is furthest from the body where muscles attach.

Meatus: A hollow tube-like opening passing through the bone where blood vessels or nerves can pass through.

Process: A section of the bone that sticks out prominently so that muscles can attach.

Ramus: Part of an irregular bone that extends like an arm.

Sinus: A hollow cavity inside a bone.

Spine: A sharp, pointy projection on a bone for muscle attachment.

Suture: The line where two bones come together.

Tuberosity: A large, rough, rounded portion of bone providing attachment for muscles.

Tubercle: A small knob on a bone providing attachment for muscles.

Trochanter: Irregular projecting area.

Types of Bones

Long bones: The tubular bones consisting of a shaft-like portion and broader ends. These are found in the upper and lower arms, the thigh and lower leg, and also in the fingers and toes.

Short bones: This term generally refers to the carpal bones of the wrists and the tarsal bones of the ankles.

Flat bones: These occur in the skull, sternum, parts of the ribs, and the shoulder blades and pelvic bones.

Irregular bones: Some of the skull bones are irregular, as are the vertebrae and other components of the spinal column.

Sesamoid bones: Small, round bones embedded in tendons around joints. An example is the patella, or knee cap.

Joints

Ball and Socket, Ellipsoidal, Saddle, Hinge, Pivot and Gliding

Ball and socket joint: A rounded head of one bone fits into a curved space on another. Examples are the shoulder and hip.

Ellipsoidal joint: A rounded projection that is oval shaped on one bone fits into a corresponding elliptical space on another bone. An example is where the radius in the forearm joins the carpal bones of the wrist.

Saddle joint: The joining portions of both bones are saddle shaped. This occurs between the bones of the thumb and is the cause of humans' opposable thumbs.

Hinge joint: The bones come together like a door hinge and only move in two directions. The knee is an example.

Pivot joint: One bone rotates on its axis in an arch on the other bone. This occurs between vertebrae in the neck and between the radius and ulna in the forearm.

Gliding joint: Two bones slide back and forth with very little movement allowed. This happens between the vertebrae and between the bones of the fingers and toes.

Synarthrosis, Amphiarthrotic and Diarthrotic Joints

The different types of joints allow different kinds and varying degrees of movement between bones. There is very little movement, if any, at a synarthrosis. The bones are situated very close together, separated only by fibrous connective tissue. The connections between the flat bones of the skull are examples of synarthrosis joints. There is slightly more space between the bones in an amphiarthrotic joint and the space is occupied by cartilage. These joints allow some limited movement. The vertebrae of the spinal column are connected by amphiarthrotic joints. Finally, diarthroses allow the most freedom of movement, and are the most common joints in the body. At these joints, the bones are held together by ligaments. They are also known as synovial joints, because the capsule surrounding the joint is filled with fluid called synovial fluid that lubricates the joint movement.

Diarthrotic, or Synovial, Joints

Diarthrotic joints are contained within a joint capsule. The capsule is made of peritoneum, the fibrous outer covering of bone, which extends beyond the ends of the bones and surrounds the joint. The inside of the capsule is line by the synovial membrane, which secretes the synovial fluid that lubricates the joint. Hyaline cartilage, also called articular cartilage, covers the ends of the bones that come together. Between these ends is a space called the joint cavity. The cavity allows the bones to move freely past each other. The bones are secured together by ligaments, which are strong, dense cords of connective tissue. Diarthroses are the most numerous joints in the body and include ball and socket, ellipsoidal, saddle, hinge, pivot and gliding joints.

Skeletal Movement

Terms Regarding Skeletal Movement:

Abduction: Movement away from the body's midline.

Adduction: Movement toward the body's midline.

Circumduction: Bone moves in a circle, narrow at one end & wider at the other, like a cone.

Depression: Lowering toward the floor.

Elevation: Rising toward the ceiling.

Eversion: Turning the sole of the foot outward.

Extension: Increases the angle between the bones of a joint, and returns the body part to its standard anatomical position.

Flexion: Closes the angle between the bones of the joint in a bending motion.

Horizontal adduction: Movement toward the midline of the body but at a horizontal elevation position.

Inversion: Turning the sole of the foot inward.

Lateral flexion: Closing the angle between lateral body surfaces, as in bending over from the waist.

Pronation: Rotation of the forearm to bring the palms face down; turning the sole of the foot inward.

Protraction: Movement forward.

Retraction: Movement backward.

Rotation: Pivoting on an axis, as in turning the head.

Supination: Moving the forearm to turn the palms up or forward.

Bones of the Skull

Coronal suture: The juncture where the bone that forms the forehead (frontal bone) meets the two bones that form the sides of the skull (parietal bones).

Cranium: Refers to the skull as a whole, which is made up of eight head bones and fourteen face bones.

Ethmoid: Bone where the olfactory nerves go through the skull; one of the head bones.

Fontanel: The place in the top of the skull where the bones come together, which is covered only by a membrane in newborns.

Frontal bone: The forehead; one of the head bones.

Inferior nasal concha: Bones in the sides of the nasal cavity. There are two of these among the face bones.

Lacrimal: Bone near the tear glands. Two of these are included in the face bones.

Lambdoidal suture: Line where the back and sides of the skull come together.

Mandible: the lower jaw; one of the face bones.

Mastoid: projections on the sides of the skull behind each ear; also called the mastoid processes.

Maxilla: the upper jaw; one of the face bones.

Occipital: the skull bone at the back of the head; one of the head bones.

Ossicles: the tiny bones in the ear. There are three in each ear.

Palatine: two bones located behind the mouth. There are two of these face bones.

Parietal: Two head bones forming the sides of the skull.

Sagittal suture: line between the two sides of the skull.

Sphenoid: located just in front of the occipital bone toward the back of the head; a head bone.

Squamous suture: lines between bones on each side of the head.

Temporal: the base of the skull. There are two of these head bones.

Vomer: the partition between the nostrils; a face bone.

Zygomatic: the two cheek bones just under the eyes, included among the face bones.

Spinal Column

The spinal column is made up of vertebrae that are separated by intervertebral disks. The spine has four sections corresponding to its natural curves. These are, from top to bottom, the cervical, thoracic, lumbar and pelvic curves, and each section has anatomically distinct vertebrae. The seven cervical vertebrae have a feature called the transverse foramen through which nerves and blood vessels pass. The first cervical vertebrae is called the atlas, and the second the axis. The rotation between these two vertebrae allows the head to turn from side to side. There are twelve thoracic vertebrae, which are distinguished by spinous processes, the points on the backs of the vertebrae that point downward. The five lumbar vertebrae are larger and heavier than the thoracic ones in order to support the weight of the body and anchor the lower back muscles. In the pelvis the sacrum is made up of five fused vertebrae, and below it the coccyx, or tail bone, is attached. The coccyx is also made up of fused vertebrae, the number of which varies from three to five.

Arm and Hand

Humerus: The upper arm bone, which attaches to the scapula at the shoulder and the radius and ulna at the elbow.

Ulna: The bone on the little finger side (medial side) of the lower arm.

Radius: The bone on the thumb side (lateral side) of the lower arm.

Carpals: The eight wrist bones. They lie in two rows of four and are attached by ligaments.

Metacarpals: five bones in the palm of the hand. There is one for the base of each finger and the thumb.

Phalanges: the finger bones. They extend beyond the palm's metacarpals. Each finger has three, called proximal, middle and distal. The thumb has two called proximal and distal.

Leg and Foot

Femur: The large, heavy thigh bone. It connects to the coxal bone of the pelvis at its head, and joins the tibia at the knee. The femur is said to be the strongest bone in the body.

Tibia: The shinbone. The larger of the two lower leg bones.

Fibia: The smaller of the two lower leg bones. It does not form part of the knee, but does form part of the ankle.

Patella: The kneecap. This is an example of a sesamoid bone, one that is embedded in tendon tissue.

Tarsals: The seven ankle bones.

Metatarsals: Five bones in the arch of the foot.

Phalanges: The toe bones. Each toe has three, called proximal, middle and distal, except the big toes which have only proximal and distal.

The Muscular System

Skeletal Muscle

The three main functions of the skeletal muscles are movement, posture and heat production. Contractions of skeletal muscles are necessary for moving parts of the body and for locomotion. Skeletal muscles work with bones and joints to produce movement. Muscle contraction is also necessary in order to maintain the body's posture, whether sitting, standing or holding any other position. Contractions to maintain balance and posture are continuous. Skeletal muscle contractions are also a key component of the body's temperature regulation system. The process by which cells break down molecules and produce heat is called catabolism. Although other cells in the body also carry out this function, skeletal muscle cells are very active and burn a lot of fuel, and thus are the major contributor to this activity.

Muscle Contractions

Fibrillation: Individual muscle fibers contract but not together. The result is a flutter without actual movement. This is an abnormal, though common, contraction.

Isometric: Muscle tension is increased while the length of the muscle is maintained, as when someone pushes against an unmoving object.

Isotonic: The muscle tension remains the same, but the muscle lengthens producing movement or force. Isotonic contractions may be concentric, in which the fibers shorten, or eccentric, in which the fibers lengthen.

Tetanic: A prolonged, hard contraction as in the case of a muscle cramp.

Tonic: A prolonged mild contraction, as in the case of those required to maintain posture.

Twitch: A sharp contraction of momentary duration resulting from a single nerve impulse.

Muscle Fiber Patterns

Strap: Muscle fibers run parallel to each other. The muscles in the front of the abdomen are examples.

Fusiform: The muscle bulges in the middle and the fibers taper together at the ends, for example, the biceps brachii.

Tricipital: The fibers divide into three sets from a common starting point.

Pennate: The muscle fibers run in a diagonal direction from a central tendon.

Bipennate: From a central tendon, muscle fibers run diagonally to both sides, for example, the rectus femoris.

Multipennate: Pennate muscle fibers run diagonally in multiple directions from central tendons, for example, the deltoids.

Triangular: The fibers taper together at one end.

Spiral: The fibers are aligned in parallel and the entire structure twists, for example, the latissimus dorsi.

Muscle Action

There are three kinds of muscle contractions that produce different movements. These are isotonic, tonic and isometric. Isotonic contractions change the length of the muscle, and are further classified as either concentric contractions, which shorten the muscle, or eccentric contractions which lengthen it. During a tonic muscle contraction the tension in the muscle increases, but muscle length remains the same. These kinds of contractions are used to hold body position and posture. Isometric contractions are also called static contractions. During isometric contractions the tension in the muscle increases but is opposed by an external force that prevents any movement. This would be the case if, for example, you pressed your hands against an immovable wall.

Muscle Function Terms

All-or-none response: The muscle cell will contract completely or not at all.

Antagonist: A muscle that relaxes when another muscle contracts to cause movement or force.

Bursae: Fluid-filled cushioning sacs between bone and any other tissue such as tendons, ligaments, skin or muscles. They are filled with synovial fluid, like a joint capsule.

Fixator: A muscle that holds part of a joint steady so that the other part can move to produce movement of the body part. Fixators are also called stabilizers.

Insertion: Where a skeletal muscle attaches to a moving bone at the far end, or distal, from the body.

Neutralizer: A muscle that works in opposition to another muscle to prevent movement.

Origin: Where a skeletal muscle attaches to a stationary bone at the end nearest, or proximal, to the body.

Prime mover: A muscle that contracts to produce a particular movement. Another term for the prime mover is agonist.

Synergist: A muscle that contracts at the same time as a prime mover.

Tendon: Connective tissue that attaches muscle to bone.

Threshold stimulus: The minimum necessary nerve impulse to produce a muscle contraction.

Muscles Defined

Abductor: Moves a body part away from the body midline

Adductor: Moves a body part toward the body midline

Biceps: Two heads

Brevis: Shortest

Deltoid: Triangular

Depressor: Produces a downward movement

Extensor: Widens the angle between two bones at a joint

Flexor: Makes the angle smaller between two bones at a joint

Gracilis: Slender

Latissimus: Widest

Levator: Producing lifting motions.

Longissimus: Longest

Longus: Long

Magnus: Large

Major: Larger

Maximus: Largest

Oblique: Diagonally from the middle

Orbicularis: Circular

Pectinate: Like a comb

Piriformis: Pear-shaped

Platys: Flat

Pronator: Turning down or backward

Quadratus: Square

Quadriceps: Four heads

Rectus: Parallel to the middle

Rhomboid: Diamond-shaped

Rotator: Moving around an axis

Serratus: Saw-tooth shaped

Sphincter: Decreases an opening

Supinator: Turning upward or forward

Tensor: Holds rigid

Transverse: Perpendicular to the middle

Trapezius: Trapezoid-shaped

Triceps: Three heads

Origin of Insertion

Shoulder and Upper Arm

Pectoralis Major

Origin: Clavicle and sternum

Insertion: Greater tubercle of the humerus

Function: Brings upper arm toward the body and across the chest (adducts)

Coracobrachialis

Origin: Scapula

Insertion: Humerus

Function: Brings upper arm toward the body (adducts); flexes the upper arm at the shoulder

Deltoid

Origin: Clavicle, spine and scapula

Insertion: Deltoid tuberosity on the humerus

Function: Moves the upper arm away from the body (abducts); both flexes and extends the upper arm from the shoulder

Supraspinatus

Origin: Scapula

Insertion: Greater tubercle of the humerus

Function: Works with the deltoid to abduct the upper arm

Infraspinatus

Origin: Scapula

Insertion: Greater tubercle of the humerus

Function: Lateral rotation of the upper arm

Latissimus Dorsi

Origin: Thoracic, lumbar and sacral vertebrae; ribs; iliac crest

Insertion: Humerus, at the intertubercular groove

Function: Medial rotation of the upper arm; also adduction and extension of the upper arm

Teres Major

Origin: Scapula

Insertion: Humerus, just beyond the lesser tubercle

Function: Medial rotation, adduction and extension of the upper arm

Teres Minor

Origin: Scapula

Insertion: Greater tubercle of the humerus

Function: Lateral rotation of upper arm

Forearm

Biceps Brachii

Origin: The coracoid process of the scapula

Insertion: The radius, on the radial tuberosity

Function: Lateral rotation of the forearm; also flexes the forearm (decreases the elbow joint angle)

Brachialis

Origin: The humerus, on the distal end (end furthest from the trunk of the body), front side (anterior)

Insertion: The ulna, on the coracoid process

Function: Flexes the forearm (decreases the angle of the elbow joint)

Brachioradialis

Origin: The humerus, on the distal end (the elbow end), to the side (lateral surface)

Insertion: The radius, to the side and above the styloid process

Function: Flexes the forearm (decreases elbow angle)

Triceps Brachii

Origin: The scapula, below the glenoid cavity; also the elbow end of the humerus, to both sides of the elbow (both lateral and medial)

Insertion: Radius, to the outside above the styloid process

Function: Extends the forearm (opens the angle of the elbow joint)

Wrist and Hand

Flexor Carpi Radialis

Origin: The humerus, on the medial epicondyle

Insertion: The second and third metacarpals

Function: Abducts the wrist; also flexes the wrist

Flexor Carpi Ulnaris

Origin: The humerus, on the medial epicondyle; also the ulna, on the olecranon process

Insertion: The carpal bones; also the fifth metacarpal

Function: Flexes the wrist; also adduction of the wrist

Palmaris Longus

Origin: Humerus, on the medial epicondyle

Insertion: In the palm of the hand, on the fascia

Function: Flexion of the wrist

Extensor Carpi Radialis Longus

Origin: The humerus, on the lateral epicondyle

Insertion: The second metacarpal

Function: Extension and abduction of the wrist

Extensor Carpi Ulnaris

Origin: The humerus, on the lateral epicondyle

Insertion: The fifth metacarpal

Function: Extension and adduction of the wrist

Extensor Digitorum

Origin: The humerus, on the lateral epicondyle

Insertion: The second, third, fourth and fifth phalanges

Function: Finger extension

Hips and Thighs

Adductor Longus

Origin: On the pubic bone

Insertion: The femur, on the back side (posterior surface)

Function: Lateral rotation of the thigh; also flexion and adduction of the thigh (moves the thigh toward the body)

Adductor Magnus

Origin: The pubis and the ischium

Insertion: The femur, posterior side

Function: With adductor longus, flexion, adduction and rotation of the thigh

Gluteus Maximus

Origin: The ileum, sacrum and coccyx

Insertion: The femur, posterior; also the thigh fascia

Function: Extension and rotation of the thigh

Gluteus Medius

Origin: The ileum, outside (lateral) edge

Insertion: The femur, on the greater trochanter

Function: Medial rotation of the thigh; abduction of the thigh (lifts leg away from the body)

Iliacus

Origin: The ileum

Insertion: The femur, on the lesser trochanter

Function: Flexion of the thigh

Psoas Major

Origin: Lumbar vertebrae

Insertion: The femur, on the lesser trochanter

Function: Flexion of the thigh

Tensor Fasciae Latae

Origin: The iliac crest, front (anterior surface)

Insertion: Fascia of the thigh

Function: Flexion and abduction of the thigh

Legs

Quadriceps Femoris

The quadriceps femoris is really four separate muscles, but they are located close together and work together to extend the leg. They share a tendon and an insertion point on the patella, or knee cap. From the patella, the tendon becomes a ligament and attaches to the top of the tibia. The four muscles that make up the quadriceps femoris are: rectus femoris, vastus lateralis, vastus medialis, and vastus intermedius. Their origins are as follows:

Rectus femoris: The iliac spine and the acetabulum of the hip joint

Vastus lateralis: The femur, on the greater trochanter

Vastus medialis: The femur, on the interior and back sides (medial and posterior surfaces)

Vastus intermedius: The femur, on the front and outside sides (anterior and lateral surfaces).

Hamstrings

The hamstrings are located on the back side (posterior) of the thigh, and are comprised of three distinct muscles. These three muscles are the biceps femoris, the semitendinosus, and the semimembranosus. Just as the quadriceps femoris work together to extend the lower leg, the hamstring muscles work together to flex the leg, extend the thigh, and rotate the leg laterally, or away from the body's midline. Their origins and insertions are as follows:

Biceps Femoris

Origin: The femur, posterior side; also the ischial tuberosity

Insertion: The fibula; also the tibia on the lateral condyle

Semitendinosus

Origin: The ischial tuberosity

Insertion: The tibia, on the medial condyle

Semimembranosus

Origin: The ischial tuberosity

Insertion: The tibia, on the medial condyle.

Feet

Extensor Digitorum Longus

Origin: Tibia, on the lateral condyle; also the front of the fibula

Insertion: Second, third, fourth and fifth phalanges

Function: Flexion (dorsal) and eversion of the foot; extension of the toes

Gastrocnemius

Origin: Femur, on the medial and lateral condyles

Insertion: Calcaneus

Function: Flexion of lower leg; plantar flexion of the foot

Gracilis

Origin: Pubis

Insertion: The tibia, on the medial side

Function: Flexion and medial rotation of the upper leg; adduction of the thigh

Peroneus Longus

Origin: Tibia, on the lateral condyle; also the fibula

Insertion: First metatarsal, first tarsal

Function: Arch support; also eversion and plantar flexion of the foot

Sartorius

Origin: Iliac spine, front (anterior) portion

Insertion: Tibia, on the medial side

Function: Both medial rotation of the leg and lateral rotation of the thigh; also flexion of the thigh

Soleus

Origin: Both the tibia and the fibula, back (posterior) surfaces

Insertion: Calcaneus

Function: Plantar flexion of the foot

Tibialis Anterior

Origin: Tibia, on the lateral condyle

Insertion: First metatarsal and first tarsal

Function: Inversion of the foot; also flexion (dorsal) of the foot

Face, Neck and Abdomen

Buccinator

Origin: Upper and lower jaws

Insertion: Lips

Function: Holds cheeks against teeth

Masseter

Origin: Zygomatic arch

Insertion: Lower jaw

Function: Closes jaw; protraction of jaw

Pterygoid

Origin: Sphenoid

Insertion: Upper and lower jaws

Function: Sideways movement of jaw; raises jaw

Temporalis

Origin: Temporal bone

Insertion: Upper jaw

Function: Retraction of jaw; raises jaw

Erector Spinae

Origin: Spinal column

Insertion: Occipital bone; temporal bone

Function: Extension and lateral flexion of spine

Scalenes

Origin: Cervical vertebrae

Insertion: First and second ribs

Function: Flexion of head; lifting ribs

Splenius Capitis

Origin: C7-T6

Insertion: Temporal bone; occipital bone

Function: Extension and rotation of head

Sternocleidomastoid

Origin: Sternum; clavicle

Insertion: Temporal bone

Function: Flexion and rotation of head

External Oblique

Origin: Lower ribs

Insertion: Iliac crest; linea alba

Function: Trunk flexion, abdominal compression

Internal Oblique

Origin: Iliac inguinal ligament

Insertion: Lower ribs; linea alba

Function: Trunk flexion, ab. compression

Rectus Abdominis

Origin: Rib cartilage; xiphoid process

Insertion: Pubis

Function: Trunk flexion; abdominal compression

Transverse Abdominis

Origin: Lower ribs; iliac crest

Insertion: Pubis; linea alba

Function: Abdominal compression

The Nervous System

Cerebrum and Cerebellum

The **cerebrum** is the biggest section of the brain, and also the uppermost. It is divided into right and left hemispheres, and each hemisphere has a frontal lobe toward the forehead and an occipital lobe at the back. The external cerebrum is composed of gray matter, which is mainly densely packed neurons. The interior is mostly white matter. The cerebrum is involved in the so-called higher functions of the brain, such as memory, reasoning, conscious thought and action, and sensory processing. It is responsible for personality and intelligence as well.

The **cerebellum** is located at the back of the brain just under the cerebrum. Structurally it has two hemispheres and a central portion, and is made up externally of gray matter and internally of white matter. The cerebellum controls the skeletal muscles and coordinates their movements. Because of its responsibility for the skeletal muscles, it also controls posture.

Diencephalon and Brain Stem

The **diencephalon** contains two major structures, the thalamus and the hypothalamus, and sits between the cerebrum and the midbrain. Like the cerebrum and cerebellum, it is made up mostly of gray matter. The thalamus is involved with the processing of physical sensations, and helps link those to emotional responses. The hypothalamus maintains homeostasis in the body with regard to temperature, water balance, emotional regulation, sleep cycles, hunger, and some hormonal actions.

The **brain stem** links the brain and the spinal cord, and is located toward the rear of the brain and below the cerebrum. It is made up of masses of nerve fibers and pockets of gray matter. It is associated with reflexes and with cardiovascular and respiratory functions. The three divisions of the brain stem are the midbrain, the pons, and the medulla oblongata.

Midbrain, Medulla, Pons, Spinal Cord

The **midbrain** is the top portion of the brain stem, and is located just behind the hypothalamus. It is associated with reflexes that cause the head and body to move according to what a person hears or sees.

The **pons** is a bulbous bundle of nerve fibers in the middle section of the brain stem. It is involved in breathing functions.

The **medulla**, also called the medulla oblongata, is the bottom portion of the brain stem. It serves as the link between the brain and the spinal cord. It controls cardiovascular and respiratory functions.

The **spinal cord** extends from the base of the brain where the nerve fibers enter and exit the skull, down to the lower lumbar vertebrae. It is divided into thirty-one sections each of which sprouts a pair of spinal nerves. These nerves are the link between the body and the central nervous system. The hollow interior of the spinal column is called the central canal, and in the brain, it joins the ventricles. It contains cerebrospinal fluid.

Cranial Nerves

The cranial nerves are identified by both a name and a Roman numeral. They are as follows:

I. Olfactory: Sensory; smell
II. Optic: Sensory; vision
III. Oculomotor: Motor; eye movements both within the eye and in the eyelids
IV. Trochlear: Motor; eye movements
V. Trigeminal: Sensory and motor; sensory perception in head and face; chewing
VI. Abducens: Motor; eye movements
VII. Facial; sensory and motor; facial expression, salivation, sense of taste
VIII. Vestibulocochlear: Sensory; hearing, balance and equilibrium
IX. Glossopharyngeal: Sensory and motor; tongue sensations including taste, swallowing, salivation, some reflexes associated with breathing and blood pressure
X. Vagus: Sensory and motor; movements for speech and swallowing, control of smooth muscle in the upper body and abdomen
XI. Accessory: Motor; vocalization, head turning, shoulder movements
XII. Hypoglossal: Motor; moving the tongue

Sensory Receptors

Sensory receptors are part of the peripheral nervous system (PNS) and convey various types of information about the environment and circumstances of the body to the PNS and thence to the central nervous system (CNS). The five kinds of receptors are **superficial, deep, visceral, special, and pain**. Superficial receptors record information on the surface of the skin and the mucous membranes regarding such things as pressure, temperature and touch. Deep receptors are located below the surface in the muscles and tendons and register pressure, vibration and position. Visceral receptors are located in organs and record such sensations as hunger or visceral pain. Special receptors are those associated with senses like vision, hearing, smell and taste. Another name for pain receptors is nociceptors. Superficial, deep and visceral receptors can all register and communicate pain.

Reflexes

Crossed Reflex: There is a reaction on one side of the body when the other side is stimulated

Extensor Thrust Reflex: If the surfaces of the hands or feet are stimulated the arms or legs extend; can be in response to pressure, as when standing

Flexor Withdrawal Reflex: Flexes the lower leg when there is pain in the foot; also called the nociceptive reflex

Intersegmental Reflex: More than one action results from initial stimulation of one sensory neuron

Monosynaptic Reflex: A sensory neuron communicates directly with a motor neuron

Optical Righting Reflex: Body position is maintained using visual sensory information

Pilomotor Reflex: Smooth muscle in the skin contracts in response to stimulation; causes the sensation of "gooseflesh"

Postural Reflex: Tries to keep the body correctly oriented when you lose your balance or slip and fall; also called the Righting Reflex

Psychogalvanic Reflex: An emotional change causes the electrical resistance in the skin to change

Startle Reflex: Muscles in the neck and limbs contract suddenly when a person is startled

Stretch Reflex: Keeps muscles from stretching to the point of tearing; an automatic contracting of the muscles when they are doing work

Tendon Reflex: A response in a muscle when its tendon is vibrated

Vasomotor Reflex: Expands and contracts the blood vessels; regulated by the sympathetic nervous system

Visceromotor Reflex: Abdominal muscles contract when there is stimulation in an abdominal organ

Spinal Nerves

There are thirty-one pairs of spinal nerves branching out from the spinal cord to perform both motor and sensory functions. Spinal nerves are associated with four plexuses, a plexus being a network of nerve fibers that occurs where spinal nerves exit the vertebral column and branch to form other nerves. The four plexuses are the Cervical Plexus, Brachial Plexus, Lumbar Plexus and Sacral Plexus. At each of these points along the spine, there is a nerve plexus to each side of the spinal column where the spinal nerves merge. The first four spinal nerves form the Cervical Plexus between the C1 and C4 vertebrae. The Brachial Plexus consists of the next four spinal nerves, between vertebrae C5 and T1. Five spinal nerve pairs associated with vertebrae T12 to L4 make up the Lumbar Plexus. The lower six spinal nerves between vertebrae L4 and S4 form the Sacral Plexus.

Nervous System Terms

Acetylcholine: Chemical substance that transfers information between neurons

Action potential: The electrical impulse that goes out from one neuron along the axon and transfers cell to cell to convey information across the body

Adenosine triphosphate: Called ATP; the molecule in which cells store energy

Axolemma: The axon's outer membrane

Axon hillock: The part of the axon that connects to the body of the neuron; generates electrical impulses

Axoplasm: Neuron cell cytoplasm

Bipolar neuron: Has one axon and one dendrite

Chemical synapse: Gap between two brain cells where chemical reactions convey information between cells

Chromatolysis: Cell damage due to overuse or some other cause

Depolarization: Changes the electrical charge in a cell membrane from negative to positive

Dopamine: One of the neurotransmitters in the brain; also has hormonal functions

Electrical synapse: The space between neurons or muscle cells where electrical charges are transmitted

Endorphin: Brain chemical produced in response to pain

Excitatory: Describes a cell that can cause an action to take place (like a muscle cell or neuron)

Excitotoxicity: When overstimulation destroys neurons

Glial cells: Support cells around neurons

Inhibitory: A function that stops or slows action

Membrane potential: The difference in electrical charge from one side of a membrane to another

Multipolar neuron: Has one axon and several dendrites

Norepinephrine: A neurotransmitter that functions chiefly in the sympathetic nervous system

Purkinje cells: Brain cells that send information out of the cerebellum

Pyramidal cells: Neurons in the cerebral cortex

Refractory period: A break between nerve impulses

Renshaw cells: Neurons that diminish or stop actions in the nervous system

Threshold: The amount of stimulation needed to produce a result

Unipolar neuron: Has only an axon

The Endocrine System

Pituitary Gland

The pituitary gland is located just under the brain and is described as having anterior and posterior lobes. The pituitary secretes a number of hormones that are crucial to the body's physiological operation. The two lobes have very different structures; the posterior lobe is almost an extension of the hypothalamus. Both lobes are controlled by the hypothalamus; however, nerve impulses control the posterior lobe, while the anterior lobe is controlled by hormonal secretions. The posterior lobe secretes antidiuretic hormone (ADH), which acts in the kidneys to slow water excretion, and oxytocin, which causes uterine contractions and milk let-down. Overproduction of ADH causes a person to be always thirsty and produce a great deal of diluted urine. Oxytocin works in a feedback loop, whereby stimulation of the nipples during nursing causes greater production of oxytocin, which in turn promotes milk production.

The anterior lobe of the pituitary gland produces seven key hormones that act in various parts of the body. They are as follows:

Adrenocorticotropic hormone (ACTH): Controls hormonal activities of the cerebral cortex

Follicle-stimulating hormone (FSH): Promotes production of ova in the ovaries and sperm in the testes; causes the follicle cells in the ovaries to produce estrogen

Growth hormone (GH): Stimulates growth and increases rate of growth of cells throughout the body

Luteinizing hormone (LH): Stimulates testosterone secretion; promotes release of ova in the ovaries

Melanocyte stimulating hormone (MSH): Promotes melanin production in the skin

Prolactin: Targets the mammary glands for milk production

Thyroid stimulating hormone (TSH): Controls thyroid secretions

Review Video: Endocrine System
Visit mometrix.com/academy and enter code: 678939

Thyroid

The **thyroid gland** is located in the neck and partially surrounds the larynx. The thyroid secretes thyroxine (T4) and triiodothyronine (T3), both of which act in cells throughout the body to increase metabolism, which involves carbohydrate breakdown and protein synthesis. T4 and T3 also promote cell growth and stimulate the nervous system. Calcitonin is another thyroid secretion. Calcitonin plays a role in regulating blood calcium levels by slowing calcium release from the bones.

Parathyroid

The **parathyroid glands** are attached to the back of the thyroid and produce parathyroid hormone (PTH). PTH is crucial to the regulation of calcium levels in the blood stream. It acts in the bones to promote calcium release, in the kidneys to stimulate calcium retention, and in the intestines to cause calcium absorption.

Adrenal Glands

There are two adrenal glands, one on top of each kidney. They are described as being composed of a medulla and a cortex, and each of these structures is responsible for particular secretions. The adrenal medulla produces epinephrine and norepinephrine. These hormones act on the sympathetic nervous system and are associated with reactions to stress, such as increased heart rate, blood pressure, blood sugar, respiration, and the slowing down of digestion.

The adrenal cortex produces four hormones, which are aldosterone, cortisol, estrogen (in women) and testosterone (in men). Aldosterone is associated with potassium and sodium regulation, and with water balance in the body. Cortisol is involved in metabolic activities of cells and regulation of inflammation. Estrogen and testosterone promote development of secondary sexual characteristics in women and in men, respectively.

Other Glands

The **pineal gland** is located between the two brain hemispheres. It produces melatonin and is stimulated by light. The function of melanin is not fully understood; however, it appears to be associated with sleep/wake cycles and seasonal patterns.

The **pancreas** is situated behind the stomach. It contains a structure called the islets of Langerhans, made up of cells classified as alpha and beta. The alpha cells secrete glucagon, which acts in the liver to promote glucose production from glycogen. The beta cells produce insulin, causing the opposite conversion of glucose to glycogen and promoting protein synthesis and the transportation of glucose and amino acids through cell membranes.

The **thymus** is located between the lungs. It produces thymosin, which supports immune function by promoting white blood cell growth. The thymus shrinks as people get older.

The **reproductive glands** are associated with reproduction and secondary sexual characteristics. The testes are located in the male scrotum and produce testosterone. The ovaries sit low in the abdomen and secrete estrogen and progesterone in the female. During pregnancy, the placenta secretes estrogen, progesterone, and gonadotropin.

The Circulatory System

Central Nervous System

The brain and the spinal cord are the two parts of the central nervous system (CNS). Both of these organs are protected by bone, the brain by the skull and the spinal cord by the vertebral column. The hollow portion of the skull where the brain sits is called the cranial cavity, and similarly the hollow inside the spinal column is called the vertebral canal. Between the bones and the CNS tissue are membranes called meninges, which in turn are made up of three layers named from outer to inner the dura mater, the arachnoid and the pia mater. The pia mater is made up mainly of blood vessels. Between it and the arachnoid layer is the cerebrospinal fluid. The arachnoid itself is so called because it is net-like. The outer dura mater is a tougher layer of connective tissue that attaches to the surrounding bone.

Peripheral Nervous System

The peripheral nervous system (PNS) is responsible for communication between the central nervous system (CNS) and the rest of the body. It includes the twelve pairs of cranial nerves and the thirty-one pairs of spinal nerves. The PNS is generally discussed in terms of two systems, the somatic and autonomic. The somatic system refers to motor neurons that are under a person's voluntary control. These neurons are involved in movement of large skeletal muscles and other conscious actions. The autonomic system also contains motor neurons, but these are not under conscious or voluntary control. These neurons have to do with the functions of organs and glands and smooth muscle tissues. The autonomic system is further divided into sympathetic and parasympathetic portions. The sympathetic system controls things like the "fight or flight" reaction, and the physical and physiological associations of stress. The parasympathetic system regulates functions of the heart, the digestive tract and other such body components known as visceral effectors. The neurotransmitter acetylcholine is associated with parasympathetic activity.

Blood

Blood is part of the circulatory system, and although it is a liquid, it is classified as connective tissue. It is composed of a liquid base called plasma that carries water, protein, carbohydrates, fats, hormones, electrolytes, gasses and a variety of blood cells. The cells carried in the blood are referred to as its formed elements. Three kinds of blood cells are erythrocytes, or red blood cells; leukocytes, or white blood cells; and thrombocytes, or platelets. All of these are generated by red bone marrow. Red cells carry oxygen and carbon dioxide through the body and are partially composed of the red pigment hemoglobin. White cells are part of the body's immune system. They attack bacteria, viruses and other intruders and form antibodies. Platelets are part of the blood clotting process.

Blood Vessels

All of these are blood vessels. They are made up of different tissues and perform specific functions in the circulatory system. Veins return blood to the heart from elsewhere in the body. They are made mostly of connective tissue, and contain valves to prevent blood from flowing backward. Only the pulmonary veins carry oxygenated blood, which they return to the heart from the lungs with oxygen for the rest of the body. All the other veins carry deoxygenated blood. Arteries carry blood from the heart to the rest of the body. They are made mostly of muscular tissue, and they carry blood rich in oxygen. Only the pulmonary artery carries deoxygenated blood, which is transported to the lungs for oxygenation. Capillaries are microscopic blood vessels that convey blood contents into and out of tissues. Material is conveyed into the capillaries from the arteries via arterioles, which are small, specialized arteries. Venules are the veins that correspond to the arterioles, and transport blood contents from the capillaries to the veins.

Structure and Function Terms

Baroreceptor: Located in the walls of arteries to detect pressure changes by sensing the walls stretching.

Interstitial fluid: Located around the outside of cells in the body's tissues; exchanges material with the capillaries.

Lumen: The hollow interior of a blood vessel.

Precapillary sphincters: Fibers of smooth muscle around the base of a capillary and where capillaries and arteries connect; control blood flow in capillaries.

Tunica externa: The outer layer of an artery or vein; primarily connective tissue.

Tunica media: The middle layer of the wall of an artery or vein; primarily muscle tissue.

Tunica interna: The inner layer of the wall of an artery or vein; a single layer of epithelial cells.

Vasoconstrictor: Anything that causes a blood vessel to contract.

Vasodilator: Anything that causes a blood vessel to expand.

Neurons

Neurons are the cells of the nervous system. They are generally classified as sensory, motor or interneurons. Sensory neurons are also called afferent neurons, and they communicate information from the peripheral nervous system to the central nervous system. Motor neurons are also known as efferent neurons, and they carry impulses from the central to the peripheral nervous system.

Interneurons are responsible for communication between the motor and sensory neurons, and are part of the central nervous system. The three major anatomical components to a neuron are the cell body, the axon and a number of dendrites. The cell body is the central portion of the cell. The axon extends away from the cell and carries impulses and information to the next cell in the nerve fiber. The dendrites are projections that bring information and impulses to the cell from outside. Motor neurons are surrounded by the myelin sheath, which is made primarily of fat and helps promote the transmission of impulses.

Circulatory Routes

The four primary systems of circulation are coronary, hepatic portal, pulmonary and systemic. Coronary circulation involves the flow of blood in the heart to the heart muscle via the coronary arteries. Hepatic portal circulation brings venous blood from the stomach, intestines, pancreas, gall bladder and spleen to the liver, and then out of the liver for return to the heart. Pulmonary circulation refers to blood flow from the heart to the lungs for oxygenation, and then back to the heart. The blood vessels involved are the pulmonary veins and pulmonary artery, as well as capillaries, arterioles and venules. Systemic circulation is the flow of blood from the heart via the arteries to all parts of the body, and its return through the veins to the heart.

Blood Pressure and Pulse

Blood pressure refers to pressure in the arteries of the systemic circulatory route. Blood pressure is greatest when the ventricles contract pumping blood out into the aorta, and lowest when the ventricles relax. The pressure during ventricular contraction is called the systolic blood pressure; during ventricular relaxation, it is called diastolic blood pressure. Blood pressure is measured in the brachial artery in units of mmHg (millimeters mercury). The optimum systolic measurement is 115, and the optimum diastolic measurement 75. The difference between systolic and diastolic blood pressure is called pulse pressure. When the artery walls expand and contract as the ventricles pump and relax, you can feel the pulse by placing a finger on a major artery.

Blood pressure is largely controlled by the autonomic nervous system, but several things can influence it. One is cardiac output, which means the amount of blood the heart can pump out with each ventricular contraction. Changes in heart rate change the cardiac output. Another is blood volume, or the amount of blood that is in the circulatory system at one time. Dehydration and blood loss are examples of conditions that alter blood volume. A third is peripheral resistance, which has to do with the friction of blood against the vessel walls. Arterioles expand and contract to control peripheral resistance. A fourth factor is viscosity, or the thickness of blood, which can increase if the concentration of blood cells and proteins in the blood goes up.

Cardiac Anatomy and Function

Atrioventricular node (also called AV node): Conducts electrical impulses between the atria and the ventricles.

Bicuspid valve (also called the mitral valve): Located between the left atrium and ventricle.

Bundle branch: Cells that conduct electrical impulses to the ventricles.

Cardiac cycle: A complete cycle of normal heart activity.

Conduction pathway: Cells that spread electrical signals through the heart muscle.

Coronary sinus: Where the coronary arteries drain into the right atrium.

Endocardium: The inside layer of the wall of the heart.

Epicardium: The outside layer of the wall of the heart.

Myocardium: The heart muscle sandwiched between the epicardium and the endocardium.

Pulmonary valve: Valve between the right ventricle and the pulmonary artery.

Sinoatrial node (also SA node): Issue that generates electrical impulses; the natural pacemaker.

Stroke volume: The volume of blood pumped out of a ventricle with one contraction.

The Lymphatic System

Groups of Lymph Nodes

Axillary nodes: A large group of lymph nodes located in the chest and under the arms. They drain the breasts and the upper chest walls.

Abdominal nodes: These lie along the major blood vessels in the abdomen and drain the abdominal organs.

Inguinal nodes: Lymph nodes situated in the groin area. They drain the legs, genitals and lower abdomen.

Pelvic nodes: Located in the pelvis along major blood vessels. They drain the pelvic organs.

Submental & submaxillary nodes: Located in the mouth, and draining the nose, mouth, lips and teeth.

Superficial cervical nodes: Glandular nodes in the lower jaw and neck that drain from the face and head.

Superficial cubital nodes (also called Supratrochlear Nodes): They are situated near the elbows and drain the forearms.

Thoracic nodes: These are located in the neck and upper chest and drain the organs in those areas.

Immune Functions

Antibodies: The chief cells of the immune system; proteins that defend the body against intruding pathogens.

Antigen: A chemical that causes an immune response.

B cells: White blood cells that produce antibodies.

Complement system: Proteins that destroy microorganisms.

Gamma globulin: A type of antibody.

Interferon: An antiviral substance secreted in the body.

Memory cells: Remain in the body after an immune response so that the body will respond quickly to the same antigen next time.

Phagocyte: Immune cells that essentially eat invading microorganisms.

T cells: Hormone-secreting cells produced by the thymus to facilitate immune functions. T-cytotoxic cells destroy infected cells and also cancer cells. T-helper cells regulate immune responses.

Tonsils, Spleen, and Thymus

The **tonsils** are large lymph nodes located in the throat area. They are situated there so that they can catch and destroy pathogens that are entering through the mouth and nose. There are three kinds of tonsils. The palatine tonsils are the ones that are commonly called tonsils in lay terms. They sit on either side of the throat. The pharyngeal tonsils are the ones people call adenoids and they are located at the back of the nasal cavity. Lingual tonsils are situated on the back of the tongue.

The **spleen** is an organ located behind the stomach in the upper abdomen. It cleans and filters blood using lymphocytes (white blood cells) to destroy damaged cells and pathogens. It also stores red blood cells.

The **thymus** is a lobed gland in the chest. In children, it is very large, but it shrinks in adulthood. It is responsible for the manufacture of T cells, and is important to the early development of the immune system.

The Respiratory and Reproductive Systems

Respiratory System

Upper Respiratory Tract

The upper respiratory tract consists of the nose, pharynx, larynx and the upper trachea. The external nose is bone and cartilage. The nostrils allow passage of air into and out of the system, and the hairs in the nostrils filter larger matter out. The nasal cavity is divided by the nasal septum, and lined with mucus-producing cells. These mucous membranes warm and moisten incoming air and trap particulate matter. The pharynx is the throat, a muscular, mucous-membrane–lined passage. The ears' eustachian tubes open into the pharynx, and air passing into and out of them equalizes pressure in the ears. The larynx is also sometimes called the voice box. Air passes through it between the pharynx and the trachea. It also contains the vocal folds. The trachea is the windpipe, and descends from the throat into the chest toward the lungs.

Review Video: Respiratory System
Visit mometrix.com/academy and enter code: 783075

Lower Respiratory Tract

The lower respiratory tract includes the lower trachea, the bronchial tree and the lungs. The trachea, or windpipe, descends from the upper respiratory tract. It is a large tubular structure that keeps its form because of rings of cartilage that support it. The trachea branches in the upper chest to form the bronchial tree, the left and right branches of which branch again when they enter the lungs. The bronchi are lined with mucous membranes and hair-like cilia that filter particulate matter out of the air. The lungs themselves are divided into lobes, the left lung having two lobes and the right three. They are composed of air sacs called alveoli, blood vessels, lymphatic vessels and connective tissue.

Structure and Function Terms

Choana: Part of the nasal cavity that filters particles from incoming air.

Diaphragm: A horizontal muscle separating the chest and abdominal cavities; up and down movements control breathing.

Epiglottis: A flap of cartilage over the vocal cords that closes when you swallow so food and liquid do not go into the bronchi and lungs.

Exhalation: Breathing out; also call expiration.

Glottis: The vocal cords, or vocal folds.

Inhalation: Breathing in; also called inspiration.

Parietal pleura: The outer layer of the membrane around the lungs.

Residual volume: The small amount of air that remains in the lungs after a full exhalation.

Total lung capacity: The amount of air in the lungs after a full inhalation.

Visceral pleura: The inner layer of the membrane around the lungs.

Vital capacity: The amount of air that the lungs can exhale after a full inhalation.

Reproductive System Terms

Amniotic fluid: Surrounds the fetus and placenta within the surrounding membrane in the uterus

Areola: Dark pigmented skin encircling the nipples on the breasts

Autosome: Any chromosome other than the sex chromosomes

Chromosome: The structure that contains the DNA in a cell

Diploid cell: A cell that contains a full complement of DNA

Endometrium: The uterine lining

Gametes: Ova (eggs) and spermatozoa (sperm)

Mammary glands: Milk-producing glands in the breasts

Meiosis: Cell division

Menarche: When menstruation begins; female puberty

Menopause: The ceasing of the menstrual cycle as women age

Menstrual cycle: The female reproductive cycle, from ovulation to the release of the endometrium during menstruation

Myometrium: Uterine smooth muscle

Perimetrium: Fluid that coats the uterus

Placenta: Tissue that forms in the uterus to connect the fetus to the mother and supply the fetus with nutrients

Puberty: The onset of reproductive capability in early adolescence

Review Video: Reproductive Systems
Visit mometrix.com/academy and enter code: 505450

The Digestive System

Alimentary Canal

Mouth: Receives food and starts the breakdown of carbohydrates and starch.

Pharynx: the throat; a muscular passageway where reflexes move food down toward the stomach.

Esophagus: Passageway from the throat through the diaphragm and into the stomach; muscular structures in the esophagus keep food from going back up the throat.

Stomach: Receives food and stores it while starting protein digestion; mixes food with gastric juice for further breakdown; absorbs some nutrients into the bloodstream.

Small intestine: Long passage between the stomach and the large intestine; consists of three parts called the duodenum, jejunum and ileum; completes the breakdown of food and the absorption of nutrients.

Large intestine: Also called the colon; reabsorbs water and electrolytes; absorbs some vitamins; accumulates waste for elimination through the rectum and anus.

Review Video: Gastrointestinal System
Visit mometrix.com/academy and enter code: 378740

Accessory Organs

Teeth: Begin the mechanical breakdown of food.

Salivary glands: Present in three groups, the parotid, submaxillary and sublingual glands; secrete saliva to start carbohydrate breakdown.

Liver: Produces bile to aid food digestion; stores iron and some vitamins; plays a role in the digestion of protein, carbohydrates and fats; removes toxins and waste products from the blood.

Gallbladder: Stores bile produced by the liver and releases it into the small intestine during digestion.

Pancreas: Produces digestive enzymes, insulin and glucagons; crucial to glucose metabolism.

Absorption, Metabolism, Anabolism and Catabolism

Absorption occurs when nutrients from food are taken into the blood stream or lymphatic system. Absorption occurs mostly in the small intestine, although some nutrients are absorbed in the stomach and colon. Because carbohydrates, proteins and fats are too large to be absorbed, they are broken down into monosaccharides and disaccharides, amino acids and fatty acids, and these units are recombined in cells to form products the body can use. Metabolism refers to all of these chemical processes of breaking down nutrients and recombining their components. The two aspects of metabolism are anabolism and catabolism. Anabolism is the building of new substances out of the digested components of nutrients. Catabolism is the breaking apart of large nutrients into their component chemicals.

Fat-Soluble Vitamins

Vitamin A is abundant in yellow and orange vegetables that contain beta carotene, and in fish oil and milk. It is an antioxidant and contributes to the health of skin cells. A deficiency of Vitamin A results in poor night vision and skin problems.

Vitamin D comes mostly from sunlight but is also found in egg yolk and cod liver oil. It promotes the absorption of calcium and phosphorus and is essential to the health of bones and teeth. A shortage results in bone disorders and bone loss.

Vitamin E is found in green leafy vegetables, whole grains and nuts. It is an antioxidant and is important in the metabolism of fatty acids. A deficiency causes nerve problems and cell damage from free radicals.

Vitamin K is available in cruciferous vegetables such as cabbage and cauliflower and also in spinach. It is involved in blood clotting and so a deficiency can result in easy bruising and excessive bleeding.

B Vitamins

Vitamin B-1 (Thiamine) comes from whole grains, eggs, nuts, yeast and some meats. It is involved in the metabolism of carbohydrates, and deficiencies cause nerve problems and the disease beriberi.

Vitamin B-2 (Riboflavin) is abundant in red meat, whole grains, eggs, yeast, beets and asparagus. It helps the body metabolize carbohydrates and protein, and lack of it causes eye and skin problems.

Vitamin B-3 (Niacin) is found in whole grains, meat, nuts, legumes and yeast. It is important in the metabolism of fat, and deficiency causes nerve problems and the disease pellagra.

Vitamin B-6 (Pyridoxine) is taken in from salmon, wheat, yogurt, corn, tomatoes and yeast. It participates in the metabolism of amino acids, and a lack of it causes skin problems on the face.

Vitamin B-12 (Cyanocobalamin) comes from organ meats, eggs and dairy products. It is involved in the production of red blood cells, and a deficiency results in pernicious anemia and nerve problems.

Biotin, Vitamin C, Folic, and Pantothenic Acid

Biotin is available from organ meats, legumes, eggs and yeast. It facilitates the metabolism of fatty acids, and a deficiency can cause skin problems, joint pain and depression.

Vitamin C is found in fruits and green vegetables. It is an antioxidant and promotes healing and the formation of collagen. A deficiency of Vitamin C results in the disease scurvy and a reduced ability to heal and fight infections.

Folic acid comes from green leafy vegetables, dry beans and some grain products. It plays a role in the production of red and white blood cells, and is crucial to prenatal neural development. Inadequate folic acid contributes to red blood cell defects and spinal cord abnormalities in newborns.

Pantothenic acid is taken in from organ meats, cereal grains and green vegetables and is involved in the conversion of amino acids and fats to glucose. A deficiency causes muscle spasms, fatigue and sleep disturbances, and digestive problems.

MINERALS

Calcium is taken from dairy products, green leafy vegetables, eggs and shellfish. It is crucial to the formation and maintenance of bones and teeth and to neuromuscular functions. Deficiency causes bone and muscle abnormalities, and the disease rickets.

Chlorine, or chloride, mostly comes from salt and as such is also available in processed foods. It plays a role in electrolyte balance and the maintenance of the body's pH and is a component of stomach acid. A deficiency causes a pH imbalance called alkalosis.

Magnesium is found in grains, nuts, soy products and seafood. It is involved in the formation of bone tissue and plays a role in muscle movement. A lack of it causes muscle spasms and tremors.

Phosphorus comes from dairy products, nuts, meat and fish. It is important to bone formation and to neuromuscular function. A deficiency results in bone abnormalities.

Potassium is abundant in meat and fish, nuts and some fruits. It plays a role in neuromuscular function, and a deficiency causes muscle cramps and irregular heartbeats.

Sodium, like chloride, comes mostly from salt. It is crucial to fluid balance in the body and is also involved in neuromuscular function. A shortage of it causes electrolyte imbalance, irregular heartbeats and muscle cramps.

Sulfur occurs in meat, fish, beans, eggs and some cheeses. It is important to the production of the energy molecule ATP and the building of proteins. A deficiency can lead to kidney stones.

STOMACH

The stomach is located in the upper left side of the abdomen. Anatomically, the stomach has four regions. The central part is called the body. The cardiac region is in the upper left near the heart. The pyloric region is adjacent to the small intestine. The fundus is the bottom of the organ. The mucus-lined stomach walls contain glands that secrete gastric juice, which mixes with incoming food to form a substance called chyme. Important components of gastric juice are hydrochloric acid, pepsin and intrinsic factor. The gastric juice of infants also contains rennin, which curdles milk and makes milk proteins more available. Pepsin breaks proteins into amino acid chains called peptides, while intrinsic factor facilitates the absorption of Vitamin B-12. The autonomic nervous system and the hormones gastrin and cholecystokinin control the production of gastric juice. Chyme leaves the stomach for the small intestine through the pyloric sphincter.

Small Intestine

The small intestine is where most digestion and absorption of nutrients takes place. It is described as having three parts, the duodenum, jejunum and ileum. The inner walls of the small intestine are lined with small projections called villi which are filled with capillaries through which absorption occurs. The intestinal walls contain glands that secrete substances to aid this process. There are specialized digestive enzymes in intestinal secretions for carbohydrates, fat and protein. Peptidase breaks protein peptides into component amino acids. Maltase, lactase and sucrase convert maltose, lactose and sucrose into glucose, fructose and galactose. Lipase acts on fat to produce monoglycerides and fatty acids. The remaining waste materials are passed into the large intestine through the ileocecal sphincter.

Large Intestine

The main functions of the large intestine are to absorb water from waste material, and prepare waste material for expulsion from the body. Bacteria in the intestine aid in this process. The large intestine has three subdivisions, the cecum, colon and rectum. The appendix is attached to the cecum as well. The appendix appears to serve no major purpose, although it is filled with lymphatic tissue and may play some role in the immune system. The inner walls of the large intestine secret mucus but absorb few nutrients. Contractions of the large intestine, a process called peristalsis, are controlled by the autonomic nervous system and propel waste products toward the rectum, where they exit the anal sphincter as feces.

Kidney

Calyx: A part of the ureters inside the kidneys that collects urine.

Hilus: An area of the kidney where veins, arteries or ureters enter or exit.

Nephron: The primary functional unit of kidney tissue, made of blood vessels and other passageways for filtering.

Papilla: A small porous structure that drains urine out of the nephrons.

Peritubular capillary: A vessel that drains the veins of the kidneys.

Renal capsule: Connective tissue around the kidneys.

Renal medulla: The central part of the kidney.

Renal pelvis: The part of the ureters that is inside the kidney and collects urine to be taken away.

Renal pyramid: The area of the kidney that contains nephrons.

Nephrons

Nephrons are the primary functional components of the kidneys for filtering blood, and consist of two structures, the renal corpuscle and the renal tubule. Each renal corpuscle consists of a glomerulus and Bowman's capsule. The renal tubule leads out of the glomerulus. The following terms and definitions describe these structures:

Afferent arteriole: A blood vessel that services the glomerulus.

Bowman's capsule: The structure encasing the glomerulus.

Convoluted tubule: The ascending arm of the U-shaped nephron.

Efferent arteriole: A blood vessel that carries blood materials away from the glomerulus.

Glomerulus: Clusters of capillaries in the nephron that filter blood.

Loop of Henle: The U-shaped part of the nephron, also called the renal tubule.

Biomechanics and Kinesthesiology

Levers

A class I lever is like a see-saw. The fulcrum, or tipping point, is in the middle, while the weight to be moved is on one end and the force to move it is applied to the other end. A class II lever has the fulcrum at one end and the applied force at the other. The weight to move, meanwhile, is somewhere between them. Class III levers reverse the positions of the force and the weight. The fulcrum is again at one end, but now the force is between the fulcrum and weight that needs to move. Extending the elbow is an example of the class I lever if your hand pushes against something. An example of class II lever action is lifting your weight up by rising onto the balls of your feet. Elbow flexion uses a class III lever action. Class III levers are the most common in human biomechanics.

Motion and Rotation

The body's planes of motion are imaginary constructs, but they are useful concepts for analyzing and discussing movement. There are three primary planes of motion: the sagittal, frontal and transverse. The sagittal plane runs front to back and divides the body into two symmetrical halves. The frontal plane runs side to side, dividing the body into front and back. Finally, the transverse plane runs horizontally through the mid- section. Additional diagonal planes occur between two others. The joints of the body rotate on their axes to produce movement in one of the planes. The axes of rotation are also three: the lateral, anteroposterior, and vertical. They correspond respectively to the sagittal, frontal and transverse planes of motion. The sagittal plane and lateral axis produce flexion and extension. Abduction and adduction occur in the frontal plane with the anteroposterior axis of rotation. The transverse plane and the vertical axis describe pronation and supination movements.

Kinetic Chain Concept

The kinetic chain concept is used to talk about movements of the arms and legs. Each limb is regarded as a chain made up of links which are the bones. Typically people talk about open and closed kinetic chain activities. When the chain relevant to the motion in question is attached only at one end, it is called open. When the chain is attached at both ends, it is called closed. An example of an open chain kinetic activity is extending the elbow to stretch the arm out in front. If, however, you extend your elbow in order to do a push-up, the motion is now a closed kinetic chain activity. During an open kinetic chain activity, the active joint operates in isolation for the most part. On the other hand, during closed kinetic chain activity, the links in the chain have a greater impact on each other.

Postural Assessment

Postural assessment is a good way to evaluate the structure and function of a number of the body's components, because so many activities are required simultaneously to maintain body position and upright movement. Posture requires balance, strength and stability of many of the body's structural components all at once. The four key concepts in postural assessment are history, observation, palpation and specialized testing. History refers to gathering information from the client about his or her health, medical history, family medical history, relevant personal history and the history of the current presenting problem. Observation means the clinician's observations of the client including how he or she moves, stands, or sits and also his or her mood and attitude. Palpation is hands-on examination of both surface and deep tissues. Finally, specialized testing might be employed to evaluate range of motion, strength or any other relevant aspect.

Postural Pathology Severity

When professionals talk about problems with posture and movement they generally assign problems to a level of severity. These are sometimes described as First, Second and Third Degree postural imbalances. Elsewhere these problems are divided into Stage 1, 2 and 3 levels of impairment. The first system evaluates postural problems in terms of the degree of hypertrophy of the target muscle and hypotrophy of that muscle's corresponding antagonist muscle. Impairment ranges from inefficient in First Degree problems through distorted in Second Degree and dysfunctional in Third. The staging system looks at tension, mobility, pain and fatigue in grading postural and movement difficulties, with each stage denoting increased impairment and client distress.

Traditional Chinese Medicine

Basics

Traditional Chinese Medicine (TCM) dates back 4000-5000 years. It interweaves anatomy and physiology with a philosophical system. Many of TCM's theories of anatomy and physiology are very different from those in Western medicine; however, TCM has contributed greatly to modern massage therapy theory and technique. TCM is based on the concepts of the opposing forces of Yin and Yang, and the theory of Five Elements which are Wood, Fire, Earth, Metal and Water. Additionally, TCM recognizes Chi, a life energy that circulates through the body through a system of channels or meridians. These play an important part in TCM diagnosis and treatment. Elemental or Yin/Yang imbalances interfere with the movement of Chi and result in pathology. Treatment restores appropriate balances and allows Chi to flow properly.

Yin and Yang

Yin and Yang are opposite but interlinked cosmic forces that influence all things. They exist relative to each other, that is to say, something is only described as Yin or Yang in comparison with something else. Similarly, nothing is totally Yin or Yang, but all things are composed of Yin and Yang aspects. Some general associations of Yin are cool, wet, slow, weak and up. Yang, on the other hand, is associated with characteristics of warm, dry, fast, strong and down, among others. The organs of the human body are associated with either Yin or Yang as well, for example, the liver is a Yin organ while the gall bladder is a Yang organ. In general, solid organs are Yin and hollow organs Yang. Because of these associations, the concept of Yin/Yang forces can be used to prescribe treatments for medical problems.

Five Elements

According to the Five Element Theory, all aspects of nature are represented by the elements wood, fire, earth, metal and water. This includes organs of the body and physiological processes. The elements are perceived to act on one another in particular ways, described as either nourishing or controlling. For example, fire nourishes earth and controls metal. Metal nourishes water and controls wood. Wood nourishes fire and controls earth. Earth nourishes metal and controls water. Finally, water nourishes wood and controls fire. These relationships are used to prescribe treatments for medical conditions. Organs associated with wood are the liver and the gall bladder. Fire organs include the heart and the small intestine. The spleen and the stomach are associated with earth, while the lungs and the colon are represented by metal. Water organs include the bladder and kidneys.

Anatomical Locations

Lung Channel (Yin, metal): Begins where the chest joins the shoulder and ends on the inside edge of the thumb. There are eleven acupoints along the Lung Channel that affect respiratory problems, sleep disturbances, some skin problems, fevers and headaches.

Large Intestine Channel (Yang, metal): Starts at the tip of the index finger and travels along the back of the hand, up the arm and neck, and ends under the nose. There are twenty points along this channel that can be used to treat abdominal pain, gastro-intestinal disturbances and fever.

Stomach Channel (Yang, earth): Starts under the eye, curves down under the nose, then to the corner of the mouth. From there it goes along the jaw, up to the hairline. It descends internally, coming out again near the collar bone and continuing downward through the line of the breast, the front of the abdomen, thigh and lower leg, and ending in the second toe. The forty-five points along this meridian treat digestive problems and general weakness.

Spleen Channel (Yin, earth): Starts on the inside edge of the big toe, goes up the inside of the leg and the outer edge of the front of the abdomen and chest, where it curves back to end near the front of the armpit. There are twenty-one points on this meridian that treat digestive problems, menstrual difficulties, apathy, some disorders of the internal organs, anemia and headaches.

Heart Channel (Yin, fire): Begins in the armpit and descends the length of the arm, over the palm to end in the little finger. There are nine points on this channel. They are used to treat anxiety and depression, heart palpitations and shortness of breath, angina, cold extremities, bad dreams, memory problems and coma.

Small Intestine Channel (Yang, fire): Begins in the little finger and runs up the back of the arm and shoulder, the side of the neck, and ends just in front of the ear. The fourteen points along this meridian treat problems of the abdominal organs and urinary disorders.

Bladder Channel (Yang, water): Begins at the inside corner of the eye and runs up the forehead, over the head, and down the neck and back parallel to the spine. From the sacrum it descends though the buttock and the leg to just behind the knee. A second branch also descends the back parallel to the spine and the first branch, and the two meet behind the knee. From there the Bladder Channel continues to the foot and ends in the little toe. This is the longest Channel and contains sixty-seven points that treat urinary disorders, back pain, fatigue and also slow pulse rate. These points can also be used to treat anxiety and stress.

Kidney Channel (Yin, water): Starts on the sole of the foot and ascend the inner leg to the groin, up the front of the abdomen and over the inner side of the breast to end around the collar bone. Twenty-seven points treat sexual dysfunction, inner ear problems, urinary disorders, back pain, and fluid retention.

Pericardium Channel (Yin, fire): Begins on the chest between the nipple and the armpit, and runs along the inner arm to end at the tip of the middle finger. Nine points along this channel treat mood disorders, irregular heartbeats, nausea, and menstrual problems.

San Jiao Channel (Yang, fire): Begins on the ring finger at the base of the nail and goes along the back of the hand, up the back of the arm to the side of the neck, and around behind the ear to end between the temple and the corner of the eye. Twenty-three points treat depression, anxiety, fevers, ear, nose and throat problems, headaches and herpes virus infections. This Channel is also called the Triple Heater or Triple Burner.

Gall Bladder Channel (Yang, wood): Starts at the outer corner of the eye and zigzags around the side of the head, up over the head and down the neck. From there, it passes in front of the arm and zigzags again as it travels down the side of the abdomen. From the hip, it descends the leg and ends on the outer edge of the fourth toe. There are forty four points along this channel. They are used to treat headaches and problems of the eyes, ears and speech. They are also used for sciatica and problems with muscles and connective tissues.

Liver Channel (Yin, wood): Begins on top of the big toe and ascends the foot, inside edge of the leg, and the side of the abdomen. It angles over to end under the breast. This channel has fourteen points that are useful in treating mood disorders, hypertension, eye and ear problems, digestive disorders, menstrual problems in women, and brain problems such as stroke, seizures and convulsions. They are also useful for muscle weakness and tremors.

Du Channel (Yang): Begins between the anus and tailbone, and goes straight up the middle of the back, over the head, down the middle of the face, and ends inside the upper lip. As the central Yang channel, the Du meridian impacts all of the Yang channels and also the Yang-associated organs of the body. The twenty six points along the Du channel can also be used to treat both anatomical and physiological problems of the spine and brain.

Ren Channel (Yin): Begins in front of the anus and runs up the middle of the front of the body, the throat, and the chin to end below the lower lip. As Du joins all of the Yang channels, Ren joins the Yin channels and organs. The Ren channel is important to all reproductive functions as well as other abdominal organ functions and problems. There are twenty-four Ren channel points.

Chakra Associations

Associations of the First, or Root Chakra

The root chakra is called the Muladhara Chakra in Sanskrit. It is located at the base of the spine at the bottom of the pelvic floor. Its energy is important to the lymphatic system, excretory functions and bones. It is also strongly associated with the pelvic nerve plexus and with the adrenal glands. The color of the root chakra is red, and its sense organ is the nose, representing smell. The emotional associations of this chakra are trust, security and survival instincts. These emotional associations are related to the element earth, which is the element of the root chakra and represented in the body by bones, flesh, and a sturdy physical base.

Associations of the Second, or Base Chakra

The base chakra is called the Svadhishthana Chakra in Sanskrit, which means the place where the Self resides. It energizes the reproductive system, including the ovaries in women and the testes in men. The aortic plexus is the associated nerve plexus. Its color is orange. The sense organ of this chakra is the tongue, so its primary sense is taste. Emotionally, the base chakra relates to sexuality and procreation and by extension to creative energies generally. The base chakra also energizes food and sex drives. The element of the base chakra is water, which is considered the source of life. Because of its association with water, this chakra is also sensitive to the phases of the moon, much as the tides of the ocean are.

Associations of the Third, or Solar Plexus Chakra

The third chakra, located at the solar plexus, is called the Manipura Chakra in Sanskrit. Manipura means the place of jewels. It governs the muscles and the digestive system, and also the endocrine functions of the pancreas. The associated nerve plexus is the celiac plexus. The color of this chakra is yellow, its sense organ is the eyes, and the primary sense associated with it is sight. Thus its emotional association is also perception. The solar plexus chakra's element is fire. According to principles of Ayurveda, the traditional Indian system of medicine, fire in this region of the body is necessary for the proper digestion of food, and numerous medical ailments result from a lack of digestive fire.

Associations of the Fourth, or Heart Chakra

The fourth, or heart chakra, is located in the center of the chest and its color is green. The heart chakra is Anahata Chakra in Sanskrit, which means unstruck. It is connected to the cardiac plexus, and influences cardio-pulmonary organs and functions. It also governs the thymus gland. Its sense organ is the skin, and its primary sense association is touch; however, touch can also mean sensations felt inside the body. The element of the heart chakra is air. The emotional associations of this chakra are love and interpersonal relationships, as well as a sense of balance. Because of its connection to the cardio-pulmonary processes, this chakra is especially important to the flow of prana, or life energy, in the body.

Associations of the Fifth, or Throat Chakra

The fifth chakra is the throat chakra, or Vishuddha Chakra in Sanskrit. It is located at the base of the throat and governs the tissues and organs of the neck and throat including the thyroid gland. The associated nerve plexus is the brachial plexus. This chakra also influences the arms. The color of the throat chakra is blue. The ears are the sense organs of the throat chakra, and its primary sense is hearing. The emotional or behavioral aspects of this chakra have to do with communication. It is also associated with creative expression. The element of the throat chakra is called akasha in Sanskrit, which means void or space.

Associations of the Sixth Chakra, Known as the Third Eye

The sixth chakra is the third eye chakra, which is also called the Ajna Chakra in Sanskrit. Ajna means command. It is located in the center of the forehead and is associated with the external head, the pituitary gland and the carotid nerve plexus. Its color is a deep indigo. The third eye does not have a physical sense organ associated with it. It relates instead to spirituality and to intellectual and emotional insight. The element of the third eye chakra is called mahat in Sanskrit, which means all of the other elements combined in pure form.

Seventh or Crown Chakra

The seventh chakra is the crown chakra, located in the top of the head. It governs the brain and the nervous system, and in the endocrine system the pineal gland. The color of this chakra is violet. Like the third eye, the crown chakra does not have a physical sense organ associated with it. It is associated with higher consciousness and an awareness of the relatedness of all things.

Pathology

Surgical Procedure Suffixes

Suffixes that are used in medical terms that refer to surgical procedures:

-centesis: Drawing fluid out of some part of the body, as in amniocentesis.

-ectomy: Removal of something from the body, as in appendectomy.

-lysis: Destroying something, as in electrolysis.

-pexy: Attaching something or fixing it so that it holds in place.

-plasty: Fixing or repairing something in the body, as in angioplasty.

-rrhaphy: Closing up a wound, as with stitches, staples, or some other method.

-scopy: looking at something, usually with a light, whether inside or outside the body, as in colonoscopy.

-stomy: Making a hole in something, or cutting an opening into something.

-tome: A tool used for surgical cutting.

-tripsy: Deliberate crushing of something as part of a surgical procedure.

Causes of Disease

Auto-immunity: Auto-immune disorders result when the body's immune system attacks the body's own tissues.

Congenital: Congenital conditions are present at birth, and may be inherited traits or result from prenatal or birth trauma.

Deficiency: Deficiency here refers to dietary deficiency that is present either because of a lack of proper nutrients in an individual's diet or because the body cannot absorb and use the nutrients the way it needs to.

Degeneration: Degeneration is a gradual wear and tear breakdown of tissue due to use or age.

Infection: Infection occurs when foreign pathogens invade the body. These might be bacteria, viruses or parasites, for example.

Neoplasm: Neoplasms are tissues that grow abnormally. They may or may not be cancerous.

Trauma: Trauma occurs when there is damage to the body as a result of injury or any other factor that disrupts the body's equilibrium, for example, temperature extremes, burns of various kinds, poisoning, and other physical influences.

Risk Factors

Five typical risk factors for disease are age, environment, lifestyle, genetics and stress. Their influences on disease process are as follows:

Age: Gradual wear and tear, a natural decrease in the efficiency of physiological processes, and an accumulation of damage all contribute to the effects of aging on the body and make the aging body less able to protect and maintain itself.

Environment: Environmental factors that contribute to health status include water and air quality and exposure to toxins. Environment also plays a role in the presence of disease-causing organisms and other pathogens.

Lifestyle: Diet, physical activity level, work environment, alcohol consumption and smoking are examples of lifestyle factors that influence health status.

Genetics: Inherited traits may predispose a person to illness or injury, or make a person more resilient.

Stress: Stress resulting from emotional, psychological or physical causes reduces the effectiveness of the immune system. Additionally, the body's hormonal responses to stress over the long term can contribute to the generation of illness or injury.

Health Status Terms

Acute: A condition with sudden onset and temporary duration.

Chronic: A condition that is continuous over a long period of time.

Diagnosis: The identification of the patient's condition, usually offered by a professional.

Etiology: The cause of a disease, or the progress of its development.

Health: An individual's status with regard to physical and mental well-being.

Pathogenesis: The way that an illness or disease comes about and progresses.

Pathophysiology: The body processes that are part of a disease condition.

Prognosis: The expected result of a disease process.

Signs: Indications of disease or illness that an outside person can observe about a patient.

Symptoms: Problems that a patient reports that may be indications of disease or illness.

Syndrome: Signs and symptoms which generally appear together and are indicative of a particular disease process.

Public Health Issues

The following are terms used for public health issues:

Endemic: An endemic disease is one that is well integrated into the environment of a particular geographical area and likely carried by many or most individuals living there.

Epidemic: An epidemic condition is present in many individuals at once, and is usually spreading from the place it first appeared into other regions. It involves a sudden appearance of the condition, or the condition is present at much greater frequency than is normal.

Epidemiology: Epidemiology is a public health field that focuses on the causes of disease and disease transmission in a population.

Pandemic: A disease that is epidemic over a very wide area is said to be pandemic.

Pathology: Pathology refers both to the study of disease and to the disease conditions itself.

Disease Process Terms

When describing the epidemiology of a disease condition, it is typical to note the **mortality**, which is the number of deaths that result from that disease, and the **morbidity**, which is the number of occurrences of the disease in the population. **Acute** disease is that which has a sudden onset and generally a short duration, for example a broken arm or a case of the flu. **Chronic** disease, on the other hand, may have a gradual onset and is present over a long term. A chronic disease may be progressive as in the case of osteoarthritis, for example. Diseases can also be classified as either structural or functional. **Structural** diseases involve pathogenic changes in the body's anatomy, while **functional** disorders involve changes in physiological processes. The following terms are regarding the process of diseases:

Aerobe: An organism that requires oxygen to live.

Anaerobe: An organism that requires an environment with no oxygen.

Anaplasia: Physical attributes of a cancer cell that indicate it is cancerous.

Antibiotic: a drug or other substance that kills microorganisms, particularly bacteria.

Antibody: Cells that are part of the body's immune system, specialized to defend against particular pathogens.

Antisepsis: Disinfection to prevent or stop the spread of infection.

Antiseptic: Something that destroys or prevents the spread of infectious agents.

Atrophy: Shrinking in a body part or tissue due to lack of use or a disease condition.

Bacteria: Single-cell living organisms, some of which are disease pathogens and others of which are necessary to human life.

Benign: Term used to describe a growth that is not cancerous or invasive, though it may grow in size.

Disease: An abnormal condition that interferes with the body's homeostasis and proper functioning.

Disinfect: Stopping the growth or spread of disease by killing microorganisms.

Exacerbation: When a disease condition is suddenly made worse, usually temporarily.

Fungus: A single cell mold or yeast organism; some are beneficial and some are disease pathogens.

Hyperplasia: Overgrowth in a tissue or of a particular kind of cell.

Idiopathic: When a condition's cause is not known.

Infection: Occurs when tissue is invaded by outside pathogens such as bacteria or a virus.

Inflammation: Part of the body's immune response, in which there is swelling and heat and sometimes pain.

Local: A condition that affects only a specific area.

Malignant: Growth that is cancerous and invasive.

Morbid: Affected by disease process.

Sterilize: Destroying pathogens in order to prevent or stop the spread of disease.

Systemic: Having widespread effects all over the body.

Virulence: The power of a pathogen to spread and cause disease.

Virus: A potential pathogenic agent consisting primarily of a piece of DNA and protein that takes over cells in the body in order to reproduce itself and spread.

Nerve Tissue Conditions

These three terms describe pathological conditions of the nerve tissue.

Neuralgia means nerve pain. Pain in nerves can be caused by injury, compression, or infection. Nerve pain can be very severe, and may radiate away from the source of the cause. Sciatica is an example of nerve pain.

Neuritis is inflammation of a nerve, which may come about due to infection or injury. Herpes zoster viral infection causes nerve inflammation, as does the condition known as Bell's palsy.

Neuropathy refers to weakness of a nerve, generally of a degenerative nature. Symptoms of neuropathy include weakness, tingling, diminished sensation, and numbness. Common causes of neuropathy include uncontrolled diabetes, vitamin deficiencies, repetitive motion injuries, and heavy metal poisoning.

CNS Conditions

These are three inflammatory conditions of the central nervous system, brought about by various causes.

Encephalitis refers to inflammation of the brain. There are a number of viral infections that can cause brain inflammation, among them HIV, herpes simplex, and certain mosquito-born organisms. Other events such as head injury or poisoning can cause brain inflammation as well.

Meningitis means inflammation of the meninges, which are the membranes that enclose the spinal cord and brain. A variety of viral and bacterial infections cause meningitis, some of which are extremely virulent and dangerous. Some parasite infestations and fungal infections can also cause meningitis. Symptoms of these disorders include headache, light sensitivity, stiff neck, and fever.

Myelitis refers to inflammation of the spinal cord, and in some cases the bone marrow. Infection is generally the cause.

Nervous System Disorders

Amyotrophic lateral sclerosis (also called ALS or Lou Gehrig's disease): A progressive deterioration of the motor neurons that leads to muscle wasting and is eventually fatal.

Huntington's chorea: A hereditary disorder with onset in early to middle adulthood, in which there is uncontrolled muscle movement, difficulty maintaining posture, and progressive dementia leading to death.

Multiple sclerosis: An autoimmune disorder in which the myelin sheath surrounding neurons deteriorates and metabolic waste products accumulate in the brain leading to progressive muscle wasting and immobility.

Parkinson's disease: Deterioration of motor neurons in the brain associated with problems in the dopamine neurotransmitter system. Signs and symptoms include a shuffling gait, mask-like facial expression, tremors, and increasing problems with mobility and muscle control.

Heart and Blood Vessel Conditions

Anemia: Inability of red blood cells to efficiently deliver oxygen throughout the body

Angina pectoris: Chest pain during exertion resulting from lack of oxygen to the heart muscle

Aneurysm: A bulge formed in the wall of a blood vessel

Arrhythmia: Irregular heart beat

Congestive heart failure: A weakened pumping of the heart, especially in the left side

Heart murmur: A problem with a heart valve, such that it does not open and close properly

Hemophilia: An inherited disorder in which the blood does not clot

Hypertension: High blood pressure

Myocardial infarction: A heart attack; heart muscle tissue is destroyed due to lack of oxygen

Rheumatic fever: Inflammation of heart muscle tissue caused by a bacterial infection

Thrombophlebitis: A blood clot that causes inflammation in the surrounding tissue

Varicosity: A weakening of the walls of a vein

Headaches

Cervicogenic headaches: Caused by referred pain from a trigger point, for example in the neck or upper back.

Chronic daily headaches: A general term for head pain resulting from various causes not otherwise classified.

Tension headaches: Result from muscular tension caused by stress or injury that decreases blood flow in the muscles of the head and neck.

Sinus headaches: Result from pressure in the sinus cavities of the skull as a result of inflammation and mucus build up in the cavity linings. These generally result from allergies, colds or flu, or sinus infection.

Vascular headaches: Also called migraine headaches; result from abnormal vasodilation and may be accompanied by aura, which most often manifests as visual disturbances. Cluster headaches are migraines that occur in close succession during a specific period of time.

Dementia

Dementia refers to any deterioration of cognitive functioning and results from a variety of injuries and disease processes. Memory loss and changes in personality and behavior often accompany loss of intellectual ability. One common cause is Alzheimer's disease, a formation of lesions in the brain associated with aging. Strokes and head injuries can also cause dementia, as can HIV infection, syphilis, brain tumors, neurodegenerative disorders, inflammatory conditions, various kinds of poisoning and multiple other causes. Treatment for dementia varies according to the cause, but many forms are not reversible and may be progressive; therefore, treatment is often palliative in nature. Some forms of progressive dementia, such as Alzheimer's disease, are slowed by medication treatment. Occupational therapy can help with some forms associated with stroke or injury.

Muscular System Problems

Problems of the muscular system are collectively called myopathies. Myalgia refers to pain in a muscle, while myositis denotes muscle tissue inflammation. Disorders of muscles usually involve either atrophy, in which the muscles shrink and diminish, or hypertonicity, in which the muscle tissue builds up or tightens abnormally. Many muscular problems have a nervous system component. For example, muscle cramps, or spasms, are often caused by an irritated nerve that sends repeated signals to the muscle telling it to contract. Other causes for muscular problems include injury, lack of oxygen to the tissue, or genetic disorders. RICE is the acronym for the components of acute treatment of a muscular injury. The letters stand for rest, ice, compression, and elevation. RICE allows the injury to begin healing before rehabilitative bodywork such as massage is initiated.

Review Video: Muscular System
Visit mometrix.com/academy and enter code: 967216

Muscle Strains

A strain is an injury to a muscle or tendon. This is in contrast to a sprain, which is an injury to a ligament. Strains are graded according to the severity of the injury, determined by the amount of tissue tearing that has occurred.

First degree: 0%-10% fiber tear with some pain and swelling but no impairment to movement or function.

Second degree: 10%-50% fiber tear, involving pain and swelling and difficulty using the injured muscle or tendon. Second degree strains may require splinting during healing.

Third degree: 50%-100% fiber tear with significant pain and swelling and complete dysfunction of the affected muscle or tendon. Some may require surgical repair.

Fibromyalgia and Chronic Fatigue Syndrome

Fibromyalgia describes a collection of diffuse symptoms including general pain and fatigue, anxiety, poor sleep, irritable bowel problems, cold hands and feet, and headaches. However, it is diagnosed by the presence of specific tender or trigger points which are sensitive areas that when stimulated cause referred pain in other areas. There are eleven tender points used to diagnose fibromyalgia. In addition to massage, stress management techniques are helpful in treating this condition. Note that tender points may also be present in other muscular disorders as well.

Chronic fatigue syndrome sometimes presents with some of the same associated symptoms as fibromyalgia, but the prominent feature is general fatigue and lack of energy. It is sometimes associated with the presence of the Epstein-Barr virus. Treatment often looks at dietary and other lifestyle factors, although some people with this condition are also treated with medications such as antidepressants or antiviral and immunosuppressant drugs, the latter if there is thought to be an autoimmune component.

Disorders of the Muscular System

Chronic Myofascial Pain Syndrome (MPS): A disorder in which there is lack of oxygen to a muscle leading to tissue deterioration and pain, followed by muscle contracture that leads to further oxygen deprivation.

Cervical Acceleration-Deceleration: Commonly known as whiplash, and most often occurring in motor vehicle crashes in which the injured person is rear-ended. Injury is to the soft-tissues of the neck and produces pain, inflammation, and mobility problems.

Muscular Dystrophy: A collection of congenital disorders in which there is progressive wasting of skeletal muscles. Some forms are mild while others, such as Duchenne Muscular Dystrophy, are fatal.

Myasthenia Gravis: A genetic, autoimmune disease that causes progressive muscle weakness generally beginning in the face muscles. It is eventually fatal.

Thoracic Outlet Compression Syndromes: Refer to an assortment of disorders of the upper extremities, caused by compression of nerves and veins or arteries. There are numerous conditions that produce these disorders.

Skeletal System Problems

Fractures

Symptoms of bone fracture include pain and swelling, muscle spasms near the fracture site, grating sounds when the fractured bone is moved, impaired movement, deformity of the limb in the case of arm and leg bone breaks, and bruising. However, x-ray is usually necessary to diagnose a fracture. Certain breaks are more common in certain populations, for example older women might have fractures of vertebrae or hips due to osteoporosis. Greenstick fractures are more likely in children whose bones are still flexible. Broken shoulders also occur more often in children, while young adult men are more likely to break arms and legs.

Fractures are described as spiral, oblique or transverse depending on the direction of the break. Nonunion, malunion, and delayed union refer to problems during healing. A nonunion is when the ends of the broken bone fail to join. In a malunion, the parts join incorrectly, leading to deformation of some sort. A delayed union is one in which the healing of the broken components takes longer than is typical.

Bone fracture terms:

Complete: Pieces of the broken bone are completely separated.

Incomplete: The bone is cracked but the pieces have not separated.

Compound (also called an open fracture): The broken bone pierces the skin.

Simple (also called a closed fracture): There is no open wound associated with the break.

Comminuted: The bone is broken into multiple pieces or splintered.

Compression: The break occurs when the ends of the bone are forced toward each other rather than separated.

Greenstick: The bone is bent on one side and broken on the other; occurs most often in children whose bones are more flexible.

Stress (also called a fatigue fracture): An accumulation of tiny micro fractures as a result of repeated impact; common in athletes.

Review Video: Skeletal System
Visit mometrix.com/academy and enter code: 256447

Dislocations

A dislocation is a joint injury that occurs when a bone is displaced from its associated joint. This is also called a luxation. A subluxation is a partial dislocation. Dislocations sometimes also involve damage to muscles, tendons and the joint capsule. The symptoms of a dislocation are very similar to those of a fracture, and sometimes x-rays are necessary to differentiate between them. Those symptoms can include swelling, deformity, difficulty moving the joint, pain, and muscle spasms. A fracture dislocation is an injury in which there is a broken bone near a dislocated joint. Sometimes dislocations can be correct by simple manipulation of the joint. Others may require surgery. Sometimes it is necessary to immobilize the joint for a time, especially if associated ligaments, tendons or muscles are injured.

Skeletal Disorders

Ankylosing spondylitis: A chronic inflammatory condition possibly with an autoimmune component. Joints in the spine calcify and fuse.

Chondromalacia patella: A deterioration of cartilage behind the kneecap leading to pain and a cracking noise when the knee is extended.

Osteogenesis imperfecta: A congenital disorder in which connective tissues do not form properly and the bones are thin and fragile even at birth.

Osteomalacia: More commonly known as rickets. A disease of children caused by vitamin D deficiency. The bones become soft and break easily.

Osteoporosis: Bone loss most often caused by hormonal changes associated with age that diminishes the body's ability to use calcium.

Osteitis deformans: Also known as Paget's disease. Bone formation and repair is impaired for reasons which are not clearly understood. This causes bone to be abnormally thin or thick. Pain, bone tumors and deformities of the skull and face bones are symptoms.

Spondylolisthesis: A displaced vertebra.

Spondylosis: Osteoarthritis of the spine.

Osgood-Schlatter Disease and Legg-Calve-Perthe Disease

Both of these inflammatory bone and joint disorders occur in children. Osgood-Schlatter Disease is deterioration at the end of the tibia where it forms part of the knee joint, and where the patellar ligament inserts. It occurs when the end of the tibia, the tibial tuberosity, is not yet fully calcified. It generally affects children between the ages of ten and fifteen. Legg-Calve-Perthe Disease is similar but happens in the hip at the head of the femur. There is deterioration at the head of the femur, but the cause of this disorder is unknown. Osgood-Schlatter Disease can usually be managed with rest and anti-inflammatory drugs. Legg-Calve Perthe Disease sometimes requires bed rest and immobilization of the hip joint.

Spinal Problems

Lordosis, kyphosis and scoliosis all refer to abnormal curvatures of the spine. In lordosis the curve of the lower back is exaggerated. Kyphosis is a over-rounding of the upper back as in a "hunchback" posture. In scoliosis, the spine curves abnormally to the right or left. These spinals deformities may be congenital, or may result from poor posture or disease or injury that weakens either the spine or the back muscles. When these conditions are severe they can lead to organ displacement. Severe cases might require surgery to correct or lessen the condition. Other musculoskeletal problems often result from spinal deformities when the body tries to compensate for balance and movement. Massage, braces, physical therapy and yoga are helpful in dealing with spinal deformity.

Disorders of the Feet

These are three skeletal disorders of the feet. Bunions start with a congenital misalignment of the big toe, which angles back toward the midline of the foot. This is associated with a collapse of the metatarsal arch of the foot. Over time, bunions form large calluses, and they can become very painful. They sometimes require surgical correction. Pes planus is better known as flat feet. This condition results from a collapse of the arch of the foot, and is best managed with exercises and orthotics. Plantar fasciitis is an inflammation of the plantar fascia, which runs the length of the sole of the foot. It sometimes occurs in conjunction with pes planus, and can be quite painful. Exercises and orthotics are the usual treatment, but sometimes corticosteroids or even surgery are necessary.

Herniated Disc

A herniated disc is a kind of injury to a vertebra in the spinal column. It is sometimes also called a ruptured disc. The interior portion of the vertebra, called the nucleus pulposus comes through the exterior portion, called the annulus fibrosis. This can result from acute injury, from repetitive motion or from general wear and tear. There are gradations of severity for herniated discs, which are called in order of increasing severity bulge, protrusion, extrusion and rupture. Massage, chiropractic and physical therapy can help with many of these conditions; however, very severe cases might require surgery. The four vertebrae most commonly herniated are C-6 and C-7, L-5 and S-1.

Joints

Osteomyelitis, Gout, Lyme Disease, and Bursitis

Osteomyelitis, gout, Lyme disease and bursitis are all inflammatory conditions of the joints. Osteomyelitis and Lyme disease are both caused by bacterial infections, the former by staph or strep and the latter by a tick-borne bacterium. Gout results when uric acid crystals form in the joints, and is for many people a recurrent condition. Bursitis is joint inflammation that most often is caused by injury but may result from infection or some other disease process. Elbows and shoulders are the joints most often affected by bursitis. Bacterial infections require antibiotic treatment, and there are specific medications to treat gout. Bursitis responds to anti-inflammatory drug treatments, braces, application of cold or heat, and changes in how the joint is used.

Osteoarthritis and Rheumatoid Arthritis

Both osteoarthritis and rheumatoid arthritis are skeletal system disorders that affect the joints. Osteoarthritis results from the aging process or from injury to the joint capsule. The joint capsule does not retain its lubricating fluid adequately, the cartilage and ends of the bones deteriorate, and the joint becomes stiff and painful. Nonsteroidal anti-inflammatory drugs, glucosamine and chondroitin supplementation, and hyaluronic acid injections are helpful, as are range of motion exercises and exercise in general. Rheumatoid arthritis, on the other hand, is a systemic autoimmune disease that causes painful inflammation of the joints, which over time may become misshapen. Some of the treatments are the same as for osteoarthritis, and corticosteroids and immunosuppressant drugs are sometimes used as well. Some forms of rheumatoid arthritis begin early in life, even in childhood.

Sprains

A sprain is an injury to the soft tissue around a joint, especially a tear in a ligament. This is in contrast to a strain, which is an injury to a muscle or tendon. Sprains result when a joint is over extended sharply or moved in an unnatural direction as when a person twists his or her ankle. Sprains are graded according to how badly the ligament is torn. A grade one sprain involves up to a 20% ligament fiber tear. A joint with a grade one sprain will still move properly, but it might swell slightly and be mildly painful. A ligament tear from 20%-75% constitutes a grade two sprain. The pain and swelling are more pronounced than in a grade one sprain, and the function of the joint is more impaired. A grade three sprain represents a 75%-100% ligament tear. The joint becomes seriously dysfunctional, unable to move properly or hold against resistance. These are serious injuries that can take a long time to heal.

Seizures

A seizure is an abnormal firing of neurons in the brain, with different results depending upon the location, cause and severity of the associated brain abnormality. Petit mal seizures involve a brief loss of awareness and/or momentary inability to move. A petit mal seizure may also be accompanied by inability to speak, or suddenly speaking nonsense. A grand mal seizure is characterized by sudden muscle contractions in the large skeletal muscles and loss of consciousness. Convulsion is another name for grand mal seizure. Grand mal seizures are usually followed by an episode of confusion and/or lack of energy. Seizures have many causes. Some are the result of congenital brain abnormalities as in the case of epilepsy, a disorder in which there are repeated seizures. Others are caused by brain tumors, head injuries, or brain trauma resulting from disease, oxygen deprivation, or poisoning. Seizures are controlled with anticonvulsant medications. Some very severe cases require brain surgery to stop seizure activity.

Vision Disurbances

Amblyopia: A loss of sharpness of vision for unknown reasons.

Astigmatism: An irregularity in the lens or the cornea that interferes with depth perception, night vision, and the ability to distinguish parallel lines at a distance.

Color blindness: A genetic disorder that causes an alteration in the retina and makes it difficult or impossible to distinguish certain primary colors. Red/green color blindness occurs only in males and is the most common form.

Hyperopia: Farsightedness; inability to focus clearly on objects close up due to the shape of the eye.

Myopia: Nearsightedness; inability to focus clearly on objects at a distance due to the shape of the eye.

Presbyopia: The farsightedness that onsets with aging.

Strabismus: A disorder of the muscles around the eye that make the eyes focus in different directions, as in crossed eyes.

Ear Conditions

All of these terms describe symptoms and conditions of the ears.

Otitis externa: Inflammation of the external ear due to injury or illness and perhaps accompanied by pain and visible redness.

Otitis media: Inflammation of the middle ear, which may include ear ache, often resulting from infection and sometimes secondary to allergies or colds and other viruses.

Otitis interna: Inflammation of the inner ear accompanied by dizziness or difficulties with balance, often caused by viral infection but sometimes of unknown origin.

Tinnitus: Ringing in the ears, with various causes.

Vertigo: Dizziness associated with inner ear problems.

Ménière's disease: an inner ear disorder involving tinnitus, vertigo, and diminished hearing. Cause is unknown.

Psychiatric Disorders

Five major groups of psychiatric disorders are affective disorders, anxiety disorders, personality disorders, psychotic disorders, and organic disorders. Affective or mood disorders are characterized by persistent or recurring abnormal mood states, such as depression, mania, or alternation between the two. Anxiety disorders include such problems as panic attacks, agoraphobia and other phobias, generalized anxiety, and obsessive/compulsive disorders. Personality disorders are persistent patterns of behaving and relating to others that cause significant difficulty in one's life. Examples are borderline and anti-social personality disorders. Psychotic illnesses are those that involve hallucinations, delusional thinking, bizarre behavior, and a disordered perception of reality. Organic disorders are disturbances of mood, behavior, or emotional function that result from injury or other trauma to the brain, as in the case of dementia.

It is important to note that these classifications describe clusters of symptoms that tend to occur together, but that there can be overlap among these categories.

Skin Disorders

The term dermatosis may be used to refer to any skin disorder. Dermatitis, on the other hand, describes the symptom of skin inflammation which might occur with various skin and other disorders. Changes to the skin are called lesions. Some skin lesions are harmless, as in the case of normal moles or freckles, while others indicate disease. Additionally, some conditions that manifest initially as skin problems are actually more systemic illnesses. For example, one of the early signs of lupus is a rash on the face. Other skin lesions are caused by bacterial, viral, fungal or parasitic infections, all of which can produce dermatitis. Massage therapists interact closely with clients' skin, so it is important for them to recognize conditions that might be contagious and/or might require medical attention.

Bacterial Skin Infections

Acne: An infection of oil-producing glands under the skin, most often on the face and back. Acne is more prominent in adolescence because the glands produce more oil at that time. However, other factors such as hormone imbalances can promote acne. The bacteria in these infections are generally bacteria that are naturally present on the skin.

Carbuncle: A staph infection that starts around a hair follicle but penetrates below the surface causing pain and inflammation.

Cellulitis: A streptococcus infection of the skin and underlying tissue, sometimes secondary to another injury and causing considerable inflammation.

Folliculitis: A hair follicle infection, usually by a staph organism.

Furuncle: An inflammatory condition that starts around a hair follicle and produces a painful swelling called a boil that may need to be drained. Several of these together penetrating deeper into the tissue form a carbuncle.

Impetigo: A skin infection caused by either staph or strep organisms and occurring mostly in children. Impetigo produces one or more seeping, crusty lesions, often on the face.

Rosacea: A chronic inflammation of skin on the face.

Viral Skin Conditions

Herpes simplex 1 and 2: Produces the lesions known as fever blisters. These occur on the lips or elsewhere close to the mouth, at the edges of the eyes, or on the genitals. The virus hibernates in nerve ganglia in the neck or at the base of the spine and becomes active in response to stress.

Herpes zoster: The condition commonly called shingles. The virus stays dormant in the body in nerve ganglia of the back until activated. When active it produces painful lesions on the trunk of the body.

Pityriasis rosea: Causes scaly patches on the skin that usually resolve on their own.

Verrucae: The condition that causes warts. The small growths, which may appear on different parts of the body, may last a couple of years. Sometimes they require removal, or a person may desire to have them removed.

Fungal and Parasitic Skin Infections

Fungal infections of the skin include athlete's foot, jock itch, yeast infections, nail fungus, sun spots and ringworm. Ringworm on the skin under a man's beard is called barber's itch. These disorders produce characteristic red, itchy or painful lesions. Sun spots are fungal lesions that result in loss of skin pigment. Some parasitic conditions that lead to skin inflammation and lesions include lice, also called pediculosis, and scabies. Scabies is causes by a tiny mite that burrows into the skin. Lice include several different species of parasites which may live on the heads, bodies or genital areas of their hosts. Parasitic conditions are usually treatable with topical applications and medicated soaps and shampoos. Many fungal infections are also treated topically, while others require oral medications.

Hypersensitivity

Atopic Dermatitis (commonly known as eczema): The cause of eczema is uncertain, but it produces itchy, crusty rashes especially around the knees and elbows. It is usually a chronic or recurring condition.

Contact Dermatitis: Caused by an allergic reaction to something that comes in contact with the skin. The results vary depending upon the type of irritant and individual reaction. Poison ivy rash is an example of contact dermatitis.

Hives: Reddened swellings caused by allergic reaction, stress, or sudden temperature changes (as when you pull off your clothing in a cold room). Allergic reactions to food, medication, or insect bites are the most common causes. Hives are generally treated with antihistamines.

Seborrheic Dermatitis: Commonly called seborrhea. This is another chronic or recurring condition in which itchy, scaly, crusting patches appear especially on the face and head. These lesions sometimes involve yeast growth, and they respond to antifungal treatments.

Malignant Tumors

Basal Cell Carcinoma: This is the most common form of skin cancer. The lesions start as firm bumps and slowly grow into open sores. If left untreated they can eventually become invasive. The tumors can usually be removed surgically. They often appear on the face, where there has been a lot of sun exposure.

Squamous Cell Carcinoma: This is the second most common form of skin cancer. These lesions are pigmented, sometimes scaly spots that eventually form open, crater-like wounds. They are quicker to invade tissue below the skin than are basal cell tumors. They often appear around the mouth or at locations where the skin has been injured in the past.

Melanoma: Melanoma is a much more dangerous though more rare form of skin cancer. The lesions begin as pigmented, irregularly shaped areas and sometimes start from a benign lesion like a mole. Melanoma spreads rapidly across and below the skin, and is fatal in about half the cases.

Skin Conditions

Blackheads: Result when an oil gland under the skin gets clogged with accumulated skin oil and dirt; may be the site of bacterial growth as well. Blackheads sometimes occur in conjunction with acne problems.

Decubitus ulcers (commonly known as bed sores or pressure sores): Result when a person is immobile for long periods of time and pressure on the skin reduces blood supply to the pressure area. Typically appear on people who are bedridden or wheelchair-bound.

Psoriasis: Hereditary skin problem in which scaly patches form especially on the elbows, knees, head and hips. Psoriasis may look similar to eczema.

Scleroderma: A connective tissue disorder that is accompanied by thickened, stiff skin. The condition is progressive. This is possibly an autoimmune disorder.

Skin Neoplasms

Actinic keratosis: The so-called liver spots or age spots that appear on the face and hands due to years of exposure to sunlight.

Angioma: A red spot on the skin that results from an overgrowth of blood vessels. Birthmarks are an example.

Keloid scar: An overgrowth of scar tissue over a skin injury. Keloids are more common in African-American than in Caucasian populations.

Lipoma: A fatty lump that can be felt under the skin.

Nevus: The common mole.

Sebaceous cyst: Soft, moveable, nonmalignant tumors.

Seborrheic keratosis: Scaly or waxy-looking lesions that resemble warts; sometimes pigmented and usually raised.

Skin tag: Small overgrowths of skin cells.

Burns

Burns are caused by heat, electricity, chemicals and radiation. Burns from any of these sources can be rated as first-, second-, or third-degree burns according to severity and amount of tissue damage. A first-degree burn affects the surface of the skin causing redness and some short-term pain. Sunburn is an example. A second-degree burn affects deeper layers of skin producing blistering and swelling and considerably more pain. A person can get a burn like this from touching a hot stove burner or from exposure to a release of hot steam from a cook pot. A burn like this might leave a scar. Third-degree burns are the most serious. These burns destroy all the layers of skin and may even damage tissue further inside the body. People get third-degree burns in car or building fires, for example. Second- and third-degree burns over large areas of the body are extremely dangerous because heat and fluid are lost rapidly and continually through these wounds.

Hand and Forearm Conditions

These are conditions of the hands and forearms.

Carpal tunnel syndrome: Results when the median nerve is compressed in the wrist, and the location narrows, where it and the carpal ligament pass through a small space together. Overuse, repetitive motion, or other processes produce inflammation around the ligament and nerve making the available space smaller. This produces tingling, numbness, pain, and impaired usage in the hand and fingers, particularly the thumb and first and second fingers.

Ganglion cysts: Benign swellings that form on tendons for unknown reasons. These can appear elsewhere in the body, but are sometimes more easily detected in the forearms where tendons are near the surface.

Palmar fasciitis: An extremely rare condition in which the fascia in the bilateral palms of the hands deteriorates due to arthritis. This condition is extremely painful.

Dupuytren's contracture: A common and painless condition in which the fascia in the palm of the hand shrinks and contracts for unknown reasons. When severe, this can cause the affected finger(s) to pull inward.

Soft Tissue Problems

These terms describe problems with muscles and associated soft tissues.

Adhesion: Occurs when collagen forms where it shouldn't, attaching two muscles or muscle to tendon. Treatment includes anti-inflammatory medication and physical therapy.

Contracture: An abnormal shortening of a muscle due to nerve damage, scar tissue, or other pathological process. Treatment includes physical therapy and anti-inflammatory or corticosteroid treatments.

Hernia: Openings or tears in muscle that allow tissue to protrude. Some of these result from injury, while others are congenital. These sometimes require surgical repair.

Shin splints (also called anterior compartment syndrome) Painful inflammation of the muscles along the front of the lower leg, usually because of overuse. Treatment includes RICE (rest, ice, compression, elevation) and anti-inflammatory medications.

CP, Neurofibromatosis, and Spina Bifida

Cerebral palsy (CP) is a congenital but nonhereditary disorder that results from damage to the parts of brain associated with motor control either before or during birth. The condition is caused by trauma, lack of oxygen, or a toxin. People with CP have varying degrees of impairment in motor control and mobility.

Neurofibromatosis is a genetic disease that causes discoloration and fibrous tumors on and just below the skin. It is considered a nerve disorder because the tumor grows out of nerve tissues.

Spina bifida is a birth defect in which the spinal column does not close up fully during prenatal development. It occurs in varying degrees of severity, and sometimes the spinal cord is fully exposed. Some cases are associated with a lack of folic acid prenatally.

CVA and TIA

A **cerebrovascular accident (CVA)** is what is commonly called a stroke. A CVA involves rupture of a blood vessel in the brain as a result of embolism, hemorrhage, or thrombosis. As a result, neurons in the area are destroyed usually because of oxygen deprivation. The effects can vary from mild to severe, and may include paralysis, weakness, loss of motor or cognitive abilities, or death.

A **transient ischemic attack (TIA)** is sometimes called a mini-stroke. Stroke-like symptoms such as weakness and motor dysfunction occur briefly and then resolve. TIAs are sometimes caused by blocked arteries leading to the brain and are associated with high blood pressure as well.

Both of these conditions are treated with anticoagulant drugs. People with TIAs sometimes have bypass surgery as well.

Endocrine System Pathologies

Pathologies associated with hypo- or hyper-secretions of the eight major glands of the endocrine system:

Adrenal: Addison's disease is hypoadrenalism, while Cushing's disease results from hyperadrenalism.

Pancreas: Decreased pancreatic function results in type 1 or type 2 diabetes. Excessive production of insulin by the pancreas results in hypoglycemia.

Pineal: Insufficient production of pineal hormone secretions can cause seasonal affective disorder (SAD).

Parathyroid: The parathyroid is involved in calcium uptake and usage. Both over- and under-secretion produce problems with bone and muscle function.

Pituitary: The pituitary controls many other glands, so problems are far ranging. Deficiency can also cause dwarfism, while over-production can lead to giantism.

Thymus: Low thymus secretions interfere with the normal function of the immune system, and predispose a person to illness.

Thyroid: Hyperthyroidism causes symptoms like anxiety, hyperactivity, bulging eyes, sweating, and sleep disturbance. Hypothyroidism produces weight gain, sluggishness, depression, and dry skin and hair.

Reproductive glands (ovaries and testes): Pathology here can cause infertility or abnormal development of secondary sexual traits.

Respiratory Conditions

Upper Respiratory Infections

Infections of the upper respiratory tract can result from viral, bacterial, or fungal infection. Allergies also cause inflammation of the upper respiratory organs. Pharyngitis is inflammation of the throat, or what is commonly called a sore throat. Glands in the throat area may swell in response to infection, which can be bacterial or viral. Thrush is a fungal infection of the mouth and throat that is most often seen in people with immune systems weakened by another condition. Rhinitis is inflammation of the mucous membranes inside the nose. Allergies and the common cold are typical causes. Sinusitis is inflammation of the mucous membranes lining the sinus cavities in the skull generally as a result of allergy or infection. Sinus infections can be hard to treat because there is little blood flow to those areas to convey antibiotic drugs. Flushing the sinuses with saline solution can help.

Lung Conditions

Asthma: A chronic condition in which there are episodes of constriction of the smooth muscles of the bronchial tubes, obstructing breathing; in some cases caused by allergy.

Bronchitis: Inflammation of the bronchia as a result of infection or a chronic condition, as for example smoking.

Chronic obstructive pulmonary disease (COPD) commonly called emphysema: The lungs form areas that lose their elasticity and become nonfunctional as a result of repeated trauma, as from smoking.

Pleuritis: Inflammation of the pleura, the membrane around the lungs, causing coughing and painful breathing.

Pneumonia: Accumulation of fluid in the lungs, usually as a result of infection. Often secondary to a prior upper respiratory infection, or in people who are bedridden or otherwise immobile.

Tuberculosis: A bacterial lung disease, which can be a chronic condition in some people.

Digestive System Disorders

Cholecystitis: Gall bladder inflammation causing abdominal pain and diarrhea, especially after eating foods high in fat. If gall stones form, the condition is called cholelithiasis. Inflammation or stones block gall bladder ducts and interfere with the digestion of fat.

Crohn's disease: Autoimmune, inflammatory condition of the intestines in which scar tissue renders parts of the intestine nonfunctional.

Diverticulosis: Formation of pockets in the intestinal wall that can trap food materials and become inflamed and infected. When inflammation occurs, the condition is called diverticulitis.

Irritable bowel syndrome (IBS): Pattern of alternating diarrhea and constipation accompanied by bloating and abdominal pain, most often associated with stress and a low fiber diet.

Lactose intolerance: Insufficiency of the enzyme lactase, making it difficult to digest foods high in lactose, specifically dairy products.

Polyps: Growths in the intestines, especially the colon, that are often a precursor to cancer.

Aphthous ulcers: Commonly called canker sores. These are painful sores in the mouth and throat that sometimes appear following some other infection or injury. The cause is unknown, but they are most likely of viral or autoimmune origin.

Esophagitis: Inflammation of the esophagus, usually related to gastric reflux. Diet and other lifestyle factors such as smoking and alcohol abuse can aggravate this condition.

Glossitis: Inflammation of the tongue. This is usually caused by nutritional deficiencies, especially of B vitamins and iron.

Hiatal hernia: A condition in which the upper part of the stomach protrudes through the diaphragm, causing heartburn and pain. In some cases this is treatable with antacids and beta-blockers, but in other cases it requires surgical repair.

Peptic ulcers: Painful irritation of the wall of either the stomach or the small intestine. The lesions may be caused by overuse of aspirin, dietary and lifestyle factors, stress, or infection by the *Helicobacter pylori* (H. pylori) bacterium.

Urinary System Conditions

Cystitis: Inflammation of the bladder due to infection. This condition is far more common in women, because the shortness of the female urethra makes it easy for bacteria to travel from the vaginal area up the urethra to the bladder.

Nephritis: Inflammation of the kidneys, usually resulting from the movement of bacteria up the urinary system from the bladder. *Escherichia coli* (E. coli) is a common infectious agent in kidney infections. In some cases, people suffer from chronic kidney inflammation.

Urolithiasis: The formation of kidney stones. The stones are made of calcium and other minerals filtered from the body by the kidneys. They generally do not cause problems unless they start to move out of the kidneys. Their presence in the passageways leading out of the kidneys causes significant pain.

Genital Organ Conditions

Endometriosis: A condition in which endometrial tissue, which normally lines the uterus, forms outside the uterus as well, causing pain and bleeding, and sometimes infertility. In some cases, this disorder requires surgery, while other cases are manageable with hormone treatments.

Prostatitis: Inflammation of the prostate gland sometimes caused by infection and other times of unknown cause. The inflammation can result in pain and difficulty urinating because swelling of the prostate squeezes the urethra.

Prostatic hypertrophy: A chronic overgrowth of the prostate common in older men. It is also called prostatic hyperplasia, and can be benign or cancerous. The condition causes difficulty urinating and predisposes the person to infection and prostatitis.

Vaginitis: Vaginal inflammation due to a variety of causes. Infection by bacteria or yeast is a common cause. In some cases, infection can spread up into the reproductive organs, a condition known as Pelvic Inflammatory Disease (PID).

Effects of Injury

Injury is one of the major causes of disease and results from trauma or infection. Injury can occur at the cellular or larger anatomical levels, but the larger injuries also cause changes to individual cells in the affected tissue. Cells cannot recover, and they die if the cellular membrane ruptures or if the cell nucleus is destroyed. Inflammation occurs in response to trauma just as it does in response to infection. The symptoms of inflammation, swelling, heat, redness, and pain result from an immune response that attacks pathogens and also removes damaged cellular material so that the body can repair itself. During repair, the body can produce new cells to regenerate tissue in some cases; in other cases, the body repairs the damage by producing scar tissue. The production of scar tissue is called fibrosis.

Effects of Neoplasms

Neoplasms are one of the causes of disease. A neoplasm is an abnormal growth of cells that usually results from defects in the cells' DNA. These defects render the cells impervious to the normal mechanisms that control cell growth. The cells form tumors that can be malignant or benign. Malignant tumors are those that can invade adjacent tissue or spread to other parts of the body. Benign tumors do not spread, although they can grow in size and become large enough to interfere with the functions of surrounding tissue. A related phenomenon is that of hyperplasia, in which otherwise normal cells proliferate until there are many more of them than necessary. Hyperplasias are often a response to some sort of ongoing inflammation or irritation to the tissue. Malignant growths on the surface of the body are called carcinomas, while those that occur in other body tissues are called sarcomas.

Temperature Related Medical Conditions

Frostbite: Occurs when the skin or underlying tissue freeze after exposure to cold. The decrease in blood flow to the affected area can cause permanent injury. Hands and feet are most commonly affected. Requires medical attention.

Hypothermia: A generalized response of the entire body to overexposure to cold. Victims become disoriented and stagger when walking. Eventually they may lose consciousness and can freeze to death. Requires medical attention.

Heat syncope: A near fainting spell caused by overheating.

Heat cramps: Cramping in muscles that are working when a person is overheated. Rest, hydrate, and do not massage the muscle.

Heat exhaustion: Body temperature goes up, and skin becomes cold and clammy. Cool the person and raise the feet.

Heat stroke: Body temperature exceeds 105 degrees. Cool the person with head and shoulders raised slightly. Call 911, or take the person to a medical facility.

Mineral Deficiencies

Conditions caused by deficiencies of the following minerals:

Calcium: Bone disorders like osteoporosis and Rickets; muscle function problems

Chloride: Blood becomes too alkaline

Chromium: Difficulty metabolizing glucose

Cobalt: Vitamin B-12 deficiency, anemia

Copper: Wilson's Disease, problems with nutrient absorption, anemia

Fluoride: Bone and tooth problems such as dental decay and osteoporosis

Iodide: Thyroid disorders, especially goiter

Iron: Anemia, low energy due to difficulty transporting oxygen in the bloodstream

Magnesium: Tremors and muscle spasms

Manganese: Diabetes, difficulty converting protein to energy

Phosphorus: Bone problems and deformities, difficulty with nutrient absorption, neuromuscular problems

Potassium: Muscle cramps and irregular heartbeat, neuromuscular problems

Selenium: Dental issues

Sodium: Electrolyte imbalance, muscle cramps, irregular heartbeat, neuromuscular problems

Sulfur: Kidney stones

Zinc: Slow wound healing, poor sense of taste and smell

Therapeutic Massage and Bodywork Assessment

End Feel

When a massage therapist applies passive joint movements to assess range of motion (ROM), he or she may find that ROM is limited in different ways and for different reasons. The type of limitation is referred to as "end feel." The following are common kinds of end feel:

Empty end feel: the joint movement is limited by the client's pain, but no clear cause is apparent.

Hard end feel: ROM is limited because bones in the joint contact each other.

Muscle spasms: joint movement stops because muscles contract suddenly.

Soft end feel: muscles on each side of the joint prohibit further flexion of the joint.

Springy block: caused by lose joint parts that move and interfere with ROM

Springy end feel or tissue stretch: soft tissues of the joint stretch and then seem to go no further.

Endangerment Sites

Endangerment sites are parts of the body where caution is necessary when applying therapeutic massage techniques because there is risk of injury to internal organs and other structures. Ten major endangerment sites and their vulnerable structures are:

Below the ear: Carotid artery, nerves, styloid process

Neck and throat: Carotid artery and jugular vein; lymph nodes and nerves

Back of the neck: Brachial plexus, veins and arteries, lymph nodes

Armpit: Nerves, arteries, lymph nodes

Abdomen: Spleen, liver, and gall bladder; abdominal aorta

Elbow: Nerves, arteries, and veins; the ulnar nerve causes the "funny bone" sensation

Upper inner arm: Nerves, arteries, veins, and lymph nodes

Femoral triangle: Major veins, arteries, and nerves

Back of the knee: Major arteries, veins, and nerves

Middle and lower back: Kidneys

Ayurvedic Body Types

In the traditional Indian system of Ayurveda, the doshas vata, pitta, and kapha correspond to specific body types that indicate which dosha predominates in the individual. Personality traits are also associated with these types. The vata type is characterized by a slender build and fluctuating energy levels. They are sometimes moody and likely to experience sleep disturbances and irregular bowel habits. Pitta types have a medium build and a temperamental personality. They are more regular in the eating, sleeping and bowel habits than vata types. They are prone to stomach upsets. Kapha types are heavy and easily become overweight. They are lower energy than either vata or pitta types. They health problems to which they are prone are those associated with inactivity and overweight, for example cardiovascular disease.

Postural Assessment Principles

Postural assessment refers to evaluating the way the client holds and carries his/her body. Problems with posture may indicate both medical conditions and causes of medical conditions. Postural assessment evaluates body carriage starting with the head and neck, and proceeds downward along the cervical, thoracic, and lumbar vertebrae. Next the evaluator examines the pelvic and hip joints, the knees and patellas, the ankles, feet, arches, and toes. Things to look for are disturbances of bilateral symmetry, how the person holds his or her head, spinal curvatures, locking of the knees, ankles that turn in or out, flat feet, or unusual gait. Postural assessment can be an important part of massage therapy assessment and treatment planning, and can provide clues to many client physical complaints.

Stages of Assessment

These terms describe the stages of assessment. History refers to collecting information about the client's medical history and conditions, family medical conditions that might indicate risks or predispositions, relevant factors such as smoking, alcohol consumption, or drug use, and a thorough description of the presenting problems. Client social history including work, relationships, and any childhood trauma might also be relevant. Observation includes anything the therapist notices about the client, including mood, gait, posture, behavioral issues, range of motion analysis, and the like. Palpation means a hands-on examination of deeper tissues, considering the muscle tone, texture, and any sensitivity on the part of the client. Specialized testing includes things like range of motion (ROM) assessment, strength testing, and any other procedures designed for assessment and diagnosis.

Specialized Tests

What the following specialized tests evaluates and diagnoses:

Adson Maneuver: Thoracic Outlet Syndrome

Ankle Drawer Test: Stability of the ankle joint

Anterior and Posterior Drawer Tests: ACL and PCL injuries

Apley Compression Test: Damage to the meniscus

Apley Test: Shoulder ROM

Cervical Compression & Traction Test: Problems with cervical discs

Clarke's Sign: Chondromalacia of the patella

Cross-Over Test: AC joint damage

Empty Can Test: Problems with shoulder movement

Gapping Test: Problems with sacroiliac joint

Hawkins-Kennedy Test: Problems with shoulder movement

Nobel & Ober Test: Tightness of the iliotibial band

Patrick's Test: Problems with sacroiliac joint; also called FABER

Piriformis Test: Compromising of the sciatic nerve

Speed's Test: Bicipital tendonitis

Straight Leg Raise: Protrusion of lumbar discs

Tennis & Golfer's Elbow Test: Nerve compression at the elbow joint

Thomas Test: Hypertonicity of the iliopsoas muscle

Thompson Test: Rupture of the Achilles tendon

Tinel's Sign: Carpal tunnel syndrome

Trendelenburg Test: Stability in the hips

Therapeutic Massage and Bodywork Application

Contraindications and Precautions

The contraindications and precautions for massage in the following conditions:

Abdominal aneurysm: Do not massage the abdomen.

AIDS: Use universal precautions; collect thorough information regarding current condition and symptoms; obtain physician clearance.

Anemia: Pressure on surface blood vessels could aggravate condition.

Atherosclerosis: Avoid the endangerment sites; massage promotes fluid movement which could in turn cause embolism.

Bleeding: Avoid the area.

Bone diseases: Bones might break easily under pressure of massage; obtain physician clearance.

Bursitis: Massage can make inflammation worse.

Cardiovascular diseases: Clarify diagnosis and obtain physician clearance.

Diminished skin sensitivity (as in diabetes or other neuropathic disorders): Be careful in application of pressure; may want to obtain physician clearance depending on diagnosis.

Fatigue: If fatigue is severe and ongoing, make sure client determines cause before proceeding with massage therapy.

Fever: May indicate infection or infectious disease; massage not recommended.

Fluid retention: Clarify reason for edema; do not use massage in cases of edema due to congestive heart failure, kidney disease, or infection.

Fractures: Avoid area.

Hernia: Avoid area.

Infectious illness: Massage may aggravate the illness and spread the disease.

Infectious skin disorders: Do not use massage when these are present.

Inflammation: Avoid the area; depending on cause, physician clearance might be desirable.

Lumps: Avoid area and recommend medical evaluation before continuing massage therapy.

Migraine: Obtain physician clearance.

Muscle injury: Avoid massage until a week after the injury.

Open wounds: Avoid the area; watch for increase in bleeding or seepage.

Pain: Try to determine cause with help of client; massage may or may not be recommended.

Skin cancers: Obtain physician clearance; avoid area; note that massage may encourage metastasis.

Substance abuse: Do not perform massage if client is intoxicated.

Varicose veins: Massage only proximal to the affected area.

Massage Defined

Massage is a therapeutic modality that treats physical and physiological ailments through various manipulations of the soft tissues of the body. These tissues include skin, muscle and connective tissues. Massage therapists use their own bodies, in particular their hands and arms, as well as tools and devices designed to enhance the tissue manipulation. Massage promotes both physical and emotional well-being. It relaxes the body, and thereby the mind and can help with conditions such as anxiety and depression. Massage can increase range of motion and flexibility, accelerates healing and immune functions, reduces pain from injuries or chronic conditions, and decreases the incidence of sports or repetitive motion injuries. A wide variety of techniques come under the general umbrella of therapeutic massage.

Individual Contributors

Contributions to the field of therapeutic massage:

James Cyriax: Cyriax is associated with promotion in the late 1970s of the deep transverse friction technique which is used to lengthen and broaden muscle fibers in order to increase flexibility and range of motion.

Elizabeth Dicke: Dicke worked in the early 20th century and was interested in connective tissue massage and its effects on the nervous system. Her approach was called Bindege webs massage.

Douglas Graham: Graham is best known for his *Treatise on Massage*, which did much to legitimize massage therapy in the eyes of the medical profession.

Albert Hoffa: Hoffa authored the instructional text *Technik der Massage* in German. His approach used brief massage sessions to address specific parts of the body.

John Kellogg: Kellogg was a late 19th century physician who wrote a book called *The Art of Massage* that provided a foundation for the evolution of the therapeutic massage field.

Mary McMillan: McMillan was an aide at the Walter Reed Army Hospital in the early 20th century, where she specialized in massage, exercise, and physical therapy. She delineated the five basic massage strokes and described how to apply them.

Johann Mezger: Mezger was a 19th century European physician who described four massage techniques and first used the French terms effleurage, pétrissage, friction, and tapotement.

M. Roth: Roth was a 19th century British physician who translated the 18th century Swedish massage texts into English.

Harold Storms: Storms pioneered the use of friction massage strokes for diagnostic as well as therapeutic ends. He worked in the mid 20th century.

George Taylor: Taylor introduced Swedish massage to the United States in the mid-19th century.

Effects of Massage

Mechanical and Physiological Effects

The mechanical effects of therapeutic massage are those that address the body's gross anatomy that is the muscles, bones and connective tissues. For example, massage is used to lengthen muscle fibers in order to promote tone and flexibility. Manipulation of muscles and connective tissues increases the range of motion in stiff joints. The pressure of massage strokes applied to the body increases blood and lymph flow through the target tissues as well.

The physiological effects of massage, on the other hand, operate at the cellular level in the body. These effects include removal of waste products from cells and tissues and increased metabolism. As blood vessels dilate, blood flow to the skin increases and skin temperature goes up. These effects stimulate relaxation in the nervous system as well as the muscular system.

Psychological and Energetic Effects

The relaxation of large skeletal muscles and nervous system processes produces a feeling of well-being in the recipient of therapeutic massage. The physiological effects, such as removal of cellular wastes and increased cellular metabolism can help a person feel more energetic and healthy in general. In this way massage is effective in reducing the physical and emotional effects of stress, and is helpful in managing anxiety and depression.

The notion of energetic effects of massage refers to theories and techniques primarily derived from Indian or Asian theoretical frameworks, in which massage is used to balance the flow of life energy within the body. These techniques are used to address emotional, physical, and physiological conditions that may result from disrupted, insufficient, or excessive energy. Shiatsu, acupressure, and chakra work are examples of energetic techniques of this sort.

Circulatory System

The pressure of massage squeezes the underlying tissues and causes the blood vessels in the area to empty and refill. This facilitates removal of cellular metabolic waste products from the tissues, and also increases the flow of oxygen and nutrients into the tissues. Manipulation and compression during massage also stimulates the lymphatic system, increasing both the production and flow of lymph. The lymphatic vessels constitute a key component of the immune system, so promotion of lymphatic functions is important to maintaining a healthy immune system, removing damaged cells, viruses, and bacteria from the body. Because of the increase in blood flow, the initial effects of massage can include increased blood pressure and heart rate; however, the longer term effects include decreased blood pressure, and certain massage techniques can decrease blood pressure more immediately. Massage can also help remove fluid that is retained in the body when there is edema or swelling due to poor circulation.

Immune and Respiratory Systems

Some of the effects of massage on the immune system are due to circulatory effects, for example promoting lymph formation and lymphatic flow, and accelerating removal of metabolic wastes and pathogenic cells from the body. However, massage also promotes immune strength by decreasing the physiological and emotional effects of stress. When a person is stressed, the endocrine and nervous systems produce higher levels of hormones such as cortisol and adrenaline. These "stress hormones" eventually begin to destroy white blood cells that are essential to immune function.

Massage reduces the production of these "stress hormones" by facilitating relaxation and decreasing anxiety and depression.

The relaxation effects of massage also help with respiratory disorders by easing tension in chest and rib muscles. Massage can also help drain fluid and remove waste products from the respiratory system in some cases.

Nervous System and Pain Management

One of the primary applications of massage to the nervous system is for pain reduction and management. Massage affects pain in different ways, depending upon the type of pain and the techniques used. Massage can treat pain at its source or change the way pain signals are transmitted between the peripheral nerves and the brain. Massage stimulates the release of hormones like endorphins and neurotransmitters such as serotonin that help the body mediate pain responses. Additionally, the stimulation provided by massage can activate a process known as gating, whereby the new incoming stimuli supersede the preceding pain impulses. Massage also relieves pain by promoting healing, increasing oxygen to the tissues, and reducing edema.

Muscular System

The benefits of massage for the muscular system possibly constitute the most common reasons people seek massage therapy. Massage relaxes tense muscles, and can relieve cramps and muscle spasms. This is helpful in situations where anxiety and stress contribute to muscle tension, as well as in cases where other conditions cause chronically over-tense muscles. Therapeutic massage helps athletes and others prevent and treat muscle soreness that results from over-exercising by helping the muscle tissue get rid of metabolic waste products that build up when the muscles are working. Massage therapy is also effective in treating pain called myofascial pain that results when nerves in muscle tissue become overactive due to injury or some other pathogenic process.

Basic Massage Strokes

Effleurage and Pétrissage

Effleurage or gliding strokes are those that move over the skin but do not compress the underlying tissues. There are several different kinds of effleurage. For example, nerve strokes involve touching the skin lightly with the tips of the fingers. Shingle strokes overlap one another. Mennel's strokes are unidirectional light strokes on the arms or legs. Effleurage is useful for relaxation, beginning and ending a therapeutic session, and in certain evaluative procedures. Deeper gliding strokes are used to lengthen and broaden muscle fibers.

Pétrissage or kneading strokes address the wide, middle part of a muscle. Skin and underlying tissues are lifted, rolled, and pressed. Three techniques are ischemic compression, fulling, and skin rolling. Ischemic compression squeezes fluids out of the tissue, which is followed by an influx of new fluid. Fulling lifts the tissue under the skin, while skin rolling lifts the skin up and away from the underlying tissue. Pétrissage is useful for helping remove metabolic wastes and increasing circulation. It can also release adhesions in the targeted muscles.

Friction, Tapotement, and Vibration

Friction strokes are those that press into deeper tissues in order to cause a release of tension in deep muscle or connective tissues. These techniques are often applied near joints in order to increase circulation there. Friction can also be used to break up adhesions. Some specific friction techniques are chucking, Storm's strokes, and Cyriax's strokes. Chucking is a way of picking up tissues and moving them along the length of an arm or leg. Storm's strokes are rhythmic compressions of large muscles. Cyriax's strokes are compressions applied perpendicular to the muscle fibers.

Tapotement or percussive strokes involve tapping, slapping or otherwise striking the flesh in order to stimulate an area, increase circulation, or promote muscle tone. These techniques can also be used for people with some respiratory conditions to release chest congestion.

Vibrational techniques use shaking or quivering strokes to relax muscles or to stimulate or soothe a particular part of the body. Vibration can be applied to an entire limb or to a small surface area.

Passive, Active, and Active Assisted Joint Movement

Massage therapists use joint movements to evaluate range of motion (ROM) and to treat conditions that limit ROM. When using joint movement to treat a client, it is very important that the limb and joint be well supported, and that the exercise or technique moves only the targeted joint. Range of motion should increase gradually; otherwise there is risk of injuring the client during joint movement treatments.

During **passive joint movements** the client is relaxed and allows the therapist to manipulate the joint. **Active joint movements** are those that the client performs him or herself under the therapist's direction. **Active assisted joint movements** combine active and passive features. The client moves the joint with some sort of assistance from the therapist.

Stretching Techniques

The following stretching techniques:

Ballistic: stretch is achieved through a bouncing motion; not often used because risk of injury to the muscle and connective tissues is very high.

Passive: a completely relaxed muscle is gradually lengthened by the therapist.

Proprioceptive neuromuscular facilitation (PNF) also known as contract-relax and as post-isometric relaxation: The muscle is stretch passively and held for ten seconds, then contracted against resistance for five seconds; this sequence repeats several times.

Reciprocal inhibition: A technique in which one muscle is stretched while the antagonist muscle contracts; used sometimes to counter muscle cramps.

Assisted static: The muscle is passively stretched and held until the resistance gives.

Unassisted static: The client stretches a muscle and holds the stretch.

Universal Precautions

Universal or standard precautions are terms that refer to methods used to protect both the client and the therapist from contagious illness. A rule of thumb to go by is to keep in mind that you might infect any client and any client might infect you. To practice universal precautions avoid any person-to-person contact with body fluids or broken skin. Avoid areas of irritated or broken skin on clients, and do not allow your own broken skin to come into contact with the client's body. Wash hands thoroughly between before and after sessions, and use fresh clean linens for each client. Keep the massage table, any tools you use, and the public restroom spotless and sanitized. During massage sessions, do not place your hands into containers of creams or lotions. Use dispensers or set out the amount to be used for a particular client ahead of time. Keep the studio clean and dusted, and avoid wearing or using scented products which might precipitate allergic reactions in some people.

Therapist's Body Posture

Use of proper posture and body mechanics is essential in order for massage therapists to carry out their work without injuring themselves. Although it appears that therapists use primarily the hands and arms while working, the force and strength must actually come from the legs and lower body. The therapist needs to have a good sense of where his/her center of gravity is located. This point is called tan tien, and is in the lower abdomen in front of the lumbar vertebrae. **Tan tien** is a focal point for strength, balance, and posture. The therapist must keep the back straight and use flexion of the knees to lower and raise his/her body. Two frequently used stances are the archer stance and the horse stance. In **archer stance**, the feet are placed one ahead of the other and aligned at an angle to the table parallel to the direction of applied force. In **horse stance**, the feet and shoulders are squared facing the table.

Exercises for Massage Therapists

These exercises help the massage therapist develop and maintain strength, posture, and balance. They are both mental and physical practices.

Centering is concentrating on the body's center of gravity, or tan tien, and learning to work from it.

Grinding corn is an exercise which involves separating the feet, bending the knees, extending the arms in front, and moving the hands in a flat oval pattern in the air. It promotes balance and mental focus as well as core strength.

Grounding is a meditative exercise in which one breathes deeply and evenly and clears the mind of distractions and negative thoughts.

In the **tree exercise**, the therapist breathes deeply and evenly while standing on one foot with the arms extended and rounded in front. This develops balance and concentration.

To practice **the wheel**, stand alternately on one foot and the other while breathing deeply and evenly and moving the hands in a large, slow circle in the air in front of the body. This exercise promotes balance, concentration, and core strength.

Draping

Draping refers to ways of covering the client and the massage table in order to keep the client warm and comfortable, protect privacy, and prevent the table surface from contacting people's skin. Different methods are applied according to room temperature, type of massage, and client and therapist preference.

Diaper draping uses a table cover and towels to cover the client's genitals and breasts (in the case of female clients). Another name for this technique is contour draping.

Full sheet draping uses a large sheet to cover the table and to wrap over the client.

Tenting is a way of lifting the sheet to allow the client to turn over without becoming uncovered or getting wrapped in the sheet.

Top cover draping uses a table cover and a large sheet to cover the client.

Massage Tables

Massage tables may be portable or not. Portable tables are necessary for therapists who travel to client homes or offices, but they can also be used in a studio setting. Non-portable tables are heavier and more stable but also more expensive. Tables are usually adjustable for height. Width is a matter of therapist preference, and often shorter therapists prefer a narrower table. A wider table will, on the other hand, accommodate a greater variety of patients. When choosing a table, consider also the material the frame is made of, the amount and type of padding, and the cover material. Vinyl covers are easy to clean and disinfect. Thicker, denser padding may prove more comfortable for the client. Frames are usually constructed of wood or aluminum, and weight and aesthetics are the primary considerations there. Additionally, there are many table accessories including bolsters, arm rests, carrying cases and dollies to make the table more serviceable.

Massage Lubricants

Things to keep in mind when choosing a lubricant include the amount of friction desired for the type of massage therapy, therapist and client skin sensitivities, and the fact that many lubricants can stain linens and clothing. Thicker lubricants will allow more friction for deep tissue work. Creams are the thickest, with lotions next and oils allowing the least friction. It is also possible to use powders like baby powder or corn starch as lubricants. Additionally, some creams, lotions and oils are presumed to have specific benefits for the skin, the underlying tissues, or the client's general health and well-being. For example, choice of lubricating oil is very important in Ayurvedic massage. Similarly, the addition of essential oils confers a dimension of aromatherapy to the massage treatment. However, some clients may have allergies or sensitivities to certain oils and other compounds, so it is important to review options and preferences with new clients.

Client Positioning

The primary consideration in positioning the client is comfort, but positioning techniques can also facilitate the therapeutic treatment in a variety of ways. For example, elevating the arms slightly on pillows will relax pectoral muscles in a client who is lying on his/her back, and thus make those muscles more accessible to the effects of massage. Elevation of legs or arms promotes fluid drainage through the veins during treatment. A bolster under the knees of a client on his/her back relaxes the lower back and can make the client more comfortable and relaxed. When treating a client in a side-lying position, a pillow between the thighs can prevent discomfort in the hips and lower back. Clients who are uncomfortable on their stomachs might benefit from some slight elevation under the chest. Overall, the client should be able to relax completely and comfortably, supported in the selected position without having to work to maintain it in any way.

Aromatherapy

The basic idea behind aromatherapy is that compounds derived from various plant materials confer benefits for physiology and emotional balance. These compounds are delivered primarily via essential oils, which may be diffused into the air and inhaled or applied to the skin and absorbed into the bloodstream. Essential oils are used in miniscule amounts, generally mixed into some kind of carrier oil. Such essential oils are sometimes added to massage oils. Essential oils have differing attributes and applications. Many are either calming agents or stimulants, while others have more specific attributions. For example, geranium oil is said to benefit menstrual problems in women. Most essential oils also carry contraindications, and many can prompt allergic reactions or skin irritation in some individuals. It is very important to know the properties, uses, and contraindications of essential oils before using them in massage therapy, and to review client history and preferences as well.

Principles of Ayurveda

Ayurveda is the traditional Indian medical system which is thousands of years old. According to ayurvedic principles, the body and mind are equally important components of the whole person and treatment must address the individual holistically. Ayurveda seeks a healthy balance of three "doshas," vata, pitta, and kapha, which represent principles of movement, digestion, and structure respectively. Imbalance among the doshas results in pathology, and treatment seeks to restore balance. Individuals are predisposed to imbalances of one kind and another and certain types of imbalance are also predominant at different times of year. Dietary and other lifestyle factors aggravate the balance of the doshas, and likewise are used to correct them. Massage therapy has long been part of Ayurveda as well, where is it used to facilitate cleansing of tissues, improved energy flow in the body, and relaxation of body and mind.

Therapeutic Modalities

The following therapeutic modalities:

Cranio-sacral: A treatment modality closely related to osteopathic principles, involving manipulation of the membranes around the brain and spinal cord in order to treat chronic pain and problems of the autonomic nervous system.

Manual lymph drainage: A technique involving pressure and specialized strokes to stimulate lymphatic flow and movement of fluid through tissues to reduce inflammation or improve drainage in people with compromised lymphatic function.

Muscle energy technique: A practice in which the client contracts the targeted muscle against resistance applied by the practitioner in order to lengthen muscle fibers, improve tone and strength, and treat muscle spasms.

Myofascial release: Uses the application of steady pressure to promote release of tension so that the therapist can work deeper tissues.

Neuromuscular technique (NMT): Originated with Stanley Leif in the early 20th century. It is an approach that assumes pathogenic factors cause pain and loss of mobility, which in turn cause further pain and neuromuscular dysfunction elsewhere in the body as the person attempts to compensate for the initial problems. NMT uses the concept of trigger points to identify sources of pain, and implements a number of standard massage strokes to alter the nerve signals that are communicating pain.

Proprioceptive neuromuscular facilitation (PNF): A strategy for improving range of motion in joints using stretching against resistance alternating with release of tension. It is also called post-isometric relaxation and reciprocal inhibition.

Alexander technique: Developed by actor Fredrick Alexander in the early 20th century. It emphasizes posture and movement especially of the head, neck and spine.

Feldenkrais: Developed by Moshe Feldenkrais in the mid-20th century, this approach uses postural and movement exercises to improve energy and self-confidence, and to unlearn unhealthy patterns of moving and thinking.

Esalen massage: An approach that combines Eastern and Western techniques and originated in California in the 1960s. It emphasizes relaxation and meditation.

Trager: Milton Trager's method of retraining the mind and body using movement and light massage to promote relaxation. Key terms are "hook up" which refers to the desired mental state of the therapist, and "mentastics" meaning mental gymnastics.

Rolfing: Based on the work of Ida Rolf, this approach promotes mental and physical balance using deep tissue work. Rolfing is also known as structural integration.

Hellerwork: James Heller's approach using deep tissue work and a form of talk therapy in eleven-week treatment periods to retune neuromuscular and emotional systems.

Lomi-lomi is body work based on traditional Hawaiian practices. It is a physical and spiritual practice, and traditionally the practitioner danced and meditated as part of treating the recipient. Lomi-lomi massage uses long, broad strokes all over the recipient's body.

Jin shi do is a modern practice developed by Iona Teeguarden. It uses acupressure and breath work to treat pain and emotional problems.

Shiatsu is acupressure treatment rooted in Asian traditions. It corrects problems with the flow of energy (chi) in the body. Chi flows along pathways called meridians, and comes close to the surface of the body at key acupressure/acupuncture points.

Tui na is an ancient form of Chinese massage based on traditional Chinese medicine. It uses massage techniques similar to modern ones, applying them to balancing the flow of energy in the body and correcting physical and emotional conditions.

Watsu is a modern practice that incorporates elements of shiatsu with the use of a water pool in which the client floats in a relaxed state while receiving treatment. Watsu is used to treat physical and emotional problems.

Reiki and Reflexology

Reiki is a form of healing energy work that was initiated by Mikao Usui and is based on Eastern spiritual principles. The purpose of reiki is to balance the flow of ki, or basic life energy, throughout the body in order to promote health, mental clarity and relaxation. Reiki students learn the skills from reiki masters, who enable them to work with greater levels of ki. In some reiki practices, the therapist lays hands on the client, and in others the hands are held just above the client's body. The practice is about energy and not about massage per se; however, some practitioners are trained in both and integrate the two modalities. Reiki can also be administered over distance.

Reflexology is based on principles similar to acupuncture or acupressure. Key points on the feet and hands are used to generate a response in remote parts of the body. The therapist massages feet and/or hands, applying pressure to the appropriate points from which to address the client's needs or conditions.

Sports Massage

Sports massage serves three basic functions. It can be used to improve conditioning and performance, to prevent injuries, and to help with recovery from injuries. Athletes often spend much of the training time performing repetitive motions that lead to development of some muscles at the expense of others. Imbalances of this sort lead to tight muscles and limited flexibility, and can promote injury. Massage can help by maintaining flexibility and helping to stretch muscle fibers that are shortened from overuse.

Hydrotherapy

Hydrotherapy means using liquid water, ice, or steam to treat illness or injury. The versatility offered by the fact that water is available in these three states is one of the reasons it has many therapeutic applications. Other characteristics of water that make it useful include that it conducts heat, will dissolve many other substances, and offers support by floating. As a heat conductor, water can transfer heat in or out of an area. As a solvent it can be used as a medium for other therapeutic substances such as salts, electrolytes, or sugars. As a buoyant medium it can be used to support weakened muscles or reduce resistance on injured or vulnerable joints. Immersion in water can also be used as a gentle pressure source to stimulate blood and lymphatic flow in order to reduce edema or promote removal of wastes from tissues.

Thermal, Mechanical, and Chemical Effects of Water in Hydrotherapy Applications

Thermal effects of water result from its ability to conduct heat. Clinicians using hydrotherapy can induce therapeutic effects by applying water warmer or cooler than the body. For example, ice reduces inflammation, while a hot water bottle will cause blood and lymphatic vessels to dilate and increase blood flow.

Mechanical effects of water result from the force of water against the skin. For example, a whirlpool or water jets might help relax tight muscles. The pressure exerted by water on the body in a pool increases lymph drainage and urine production. The use of water to flush an area of the body is another mechanical application.

Chemical effects of water are those caused by using water inside the body. Drinking water to increase hydration is one example. The use of enemas to cleanse the bowel is another.

Convection, Conduction, and Conversion

Convection, conduction, and conversion are all methods of applying the thermal effects of water in hydrotherapy treatments. **Convection** refers to the transfer of heat via moving water or air, like when hot water from a boiler runs through a steam or hot water heating system. **Conduction** means the transfer of heat from one place to another through direct contact of two surfaces. An example of this would be sitting in a hot tub or placing an ice pack on an injury. **Conversion** means converting one form of energy to another. For example, when ultrasound waves pass through tissues, they are heated slightly. The ultrasound waves are converted to heat energy. Clinicians using hydrotherapy make use of these three general principles of heat transfer when drawing upon the thermal effects of water.

Effects of Heat

At the site where heat is applied, it relaxes muscles and connective tissues and causes fascia to contract. Capillaries dilate, and circulation increases in the area. Heat will reduce pain in a localized area also. While metabolism increases within cells in an area where heat is applied, the body's reaction to more generalized heat is to decrease metabolic activity. For the body as a whole, heat is also sedating and raises the heart rate. When the body is hot, the production of digestive enzymes goes up, and contractions in the gut increase.

When heat is applied to one part of the body for a prolonged period, there are effects elsewhere in the body that are called reflex effects. For example, heat applied to the abdomen will first relax the larger skeletal muscles there, and then cause stomach acid production and intestinal peristalsis to slow down. Reflex effects happen when the nervous system is stimulated at the point of heat application and sends signals to other body parts.

Effects of Cold

When cold is applied to an area of the body, the local capillaries contract and blood flow decreases. When that happens, the metabolic activity in the local cells also slows down. Muscles in the area contract, and nerve signals are inhibited. This latter response causes the numbing effects of cold. The overall body experiences the effects of cold as sedating, decreasing heart rate, and increasing metabolism.

Cold applied to one area stimulates the nervous system to send signals to other body parts, and in this way cold exposure can produce reflex effects as well. For example, application of cold to the hands will contract the blood vessels that go to the brain and decrease their blood flow.

Therapeutic Procedures

The purposes of the following therapeutic procedures:

Alcohol rub: Applying alcohol to the surface of the body to lower body temperature, cool down after applications of heat, and clean the skin.

Local application: Refers to the use of heat and cold applied alternately to relieve pain and promote healing. The alternation of heat and cold both stimulates circulation and reduces swelling. Heat/cold are applied in a 3/1 ratio.

Fomentation: The use of moist heat on the surface of the body. Fomentation produces relaxation, pain relief, and increased blood flow.

Hubbard tank: A tub of warm agitated water in which the client can fully immerse. The Hubbard tank is used to treat inflammatory and neuromuscular problems. It is also relaxing and can be of use for patients who have limited mobility, strength or range of motion when exercising.

Brand bath: Immersion in cold water accompanied by rubbing the skin. This can reduce fever and also activate the immune system.

Hot foot bath: Soaking the feet and ankles in hot water. The water temperature should be between 100 and 115 degrees. The hot foot bath not only produces the effects expected with local heat application, such as relaxation and pain relief, but also decongests the head and sinuses and produces sweating across the entire body.

Neutral bath: Immersion in water that is approximately body temperature. The neutral bath is sedating and relaxing.

Paraffin bath: Dipping a body part in hot melted paraffin. Paraffin baths make the skin soft and smooth, and are effective in reducing the pain of arthritis in joints of the hands and feet.

Whirlpool bath: Immersion in a tub with aerated water jets to agitate the water for a massaging effect on the body. Whirlpool baths promote healing of both external and internal injuries as well as relaxing the muscles and relieving pain.

Hydrocollator: A chemical pack containing silica gel used to apply moist heat to an area of the body surface for pain relief, relaxation of muscle spasms, and increased blood flow.

Ice massage: Application of ice with pressure and circular motion to create a counter-stimulus that reduces pain. Ice massage can also improve muscle tone, and it is often used in conjunction with trigger points.

Ice pack: Application of cold to a body part in order to relieve pain and reduce inflammation in the treatment of injuries and inflammatory conditions. There should always be a barrier between the ice and the skin.

Salt glow: Rubbing the skin with water and salt. The salt glow exfoliates dead skin cells, softens and smoothes the skin, and stimulates blood flow to the surface.

Russian bath: Steam application in which the patient lies in a steam box with his/her head sticking out. This treatment raises pulse, blood pressure, and body temperature. It also dilates the capillaries and other vessels, produces sweating, and increases metabolic activity. It is generally used to treat inflammatory conditions, but has also been applied to obesity and addictions. This is a potentially dangerous application, and should not be used on persons with high blood pressure, diabetes, heart disease, or circulatory problems.

Sitz bath: A tub soaking of the pelvic region, using a hot, cold, or alternating hot/cold environment. Hot sitz baths are used to increase circulation and relieve pain in cases of urinary tract infection, prostate inflammation, pelvic inflammatory disease and after certain surgical procedures involving the urethra or rectum. Cold sitz is used to tone pelvic muscles and reduce bleeding either vaginally or rectally. Alternating hot/cold sitz combines the toning effects of cold sitz with the increased circulation produced by hot sitz.

Heliotherapy

Heliotherapy is light therapy in which the body or a specific part of the body is exposed to a light source in order to treat a disorder. Three common types of light that are used therapeutically are electric or radiant light, ultraviolet light, and infrared light. Radiant, electric light is applied using a typical incandescent light bulb held a short distance from the site of treatment. The bulb produces warmth as well as light and is often used for just that reason. Ultraviolet light is applied similarly but for very short periods of time. It is used to sterilize an area or treat bacterial or fungal infections of the skin. Infrared light is experienced primarily as heat, and is used in treatment to promote relaxation or increase range of motion. When using these kinds of treatments, it is very important not to exceed the prescribed time limits for exposure. Additionally, these kinds of treatments are generally contraindicated for patients with diabetes or other conditions that cause poor circulation and decreased sensory perception.

Pain Management

Pain, especially chronic pain, leads to a great deal of physical and emotional stress. Stress in turn can aggravate pain conditions by causing muscle tension and physiological changes associated with the endocrine system's responses to stress. The risk for developing depression is also high in people with chronic pain or chronic illness. Practices like breathing techniques, visualization, progressive relaxation, and other stress management tools can help reduce the effects of stress and also improve a patient's ability to cope with pain. Numerous clinical studies have demonstrated the efficacy of mindfulness meditation, biofeedback, and stress reduction strategies in reducing pain and improving coping skills. These tools allow patients to maintain quality of life with fewer medications and fewer doctor visits.

First Aid

Just as the phrase describes, first aid is care given to an injured or acutely ill person while waiting for medical attention. First aid can stabilize or maintain the victim of illness or injury until emergency medical personnel arrive or until the person can get to a medical facility. Massage therapists may be responsible to provide first aid to clients if they become ill or are injured during a session or while they are at the massage studio. When preparing to administer first aid, make sure you have the person's consent or the consent of a legally responsible person who is accompanying them. If the victim is unconscious and no one else is present to give consent, proceed with first aid. Remember to call 911 for emergency assistance as early as possible in the process.

Primary and Secondary Survey

The primary survey looks for conditions that may be immediately life threatening such as breathing, bleeding, and cardiovascular function. The phrase ABCs of first aid refers to Airway, Breathing, Circulation, and Hemorrhage as the points to check in the primary survey. When the primary survey is complete, proceed with the secondary survey, which involves a thorough check of the victim from head to toe to look for any other signs and symptoms. The findings might include swelling, pain, bruising, and the like. Be sure to check also for any medical alert tags the person might be wearing. If the person is conscious and communicative, ask him or her about any pain, other medical conditions, medications they are taking, or any other relevant information.

Cardiopulmonary Resuscitation

Cardiopulmonary resuscitation (CPR) is used to save the lives of people who have stopped breathing or whose hearts have stopped beating. Examples include heart attack and drowning. The two components of CPR are mouth-to-mouth breathing and chest compression. Individuals must be trained and certified in proper CPR technique. The first thing to do is call 911 for emergency medical service. Then proceed with CPR. The steps of CPR are abbreviated by the following letters:

R = Responsiveness (check the victim for responsiveness)
A = Actuate EMS system (call 911)
P = Position (place the victim on his/her back)
A = Airway (tilt the victim's head back and lift chin to open the airway)
B = Breathing (check to see if the victim is breathing)
B = Breaths (administer two mouth to mouth breaths)
C = Circulation (check carotid artery for pulse)
C = Chest (administer chest compressions if there is no pulse)

CPR

Common complications of CPR include vomiting, accumulation of air in the stomach, inhalation of fluid or other foreign matter, and bruised or broken ribs. Recommended procedures are as follows:

Vomiting: Roll victim onto his/her side and keep the mouth cleared out to prevent choking.

Air in the stomach: Use mouth to nose rather than mouth to mouth breathing; make sure the airway is open to the lungs. If there is air in the stomach, the stomach will enlarge and distend.

Rib and chest injuries: Be careful of hand position during chest compressions and use smooth rather than abrupt strokes. Rib and chest injuries can easily result from the chest compressions of CPR, especially in older or frail people.

Choking

A person who is choking may be unable to speak, breath, or cough; however, they should be able to nod when you ask if they are choking. The first thing to do is call 911, or have some else who is present call. The procedure for expelling an object from a choking person's throat is the Heimlich maneuver, in which abdominal thrusts are applied to the victim, generally with the victim's back to the person administering the thrusts. A general rule is to administer five thrusts at a time and then check the victim's status. The Heimlich maneuver is intended to dislodge a foreign object so that the person can breathe and cough. If a choking victim is unconscious, clear out the mouth, open the airway, and administer mouth to mouth breathing. Use full CPR if the victim's heart stops (indicated by a lack of pulse). When infants or small children choke, the procedure is to tip the child forward and deliver several sharp blows to the upper middle back in order to expel the object.

Anaphylactic and Hypovolemic Shock

Anaphylactic shock occurs when a person experiences a severe allergic reaction. This is a life-threatening condition. Symptoms begin with coughing, sneezing, and rash or hives. Swelling in the face, mouth, and neck area causes difficulty breathing and chest tightness. There may also be nausea and vomiting, dizziness, and abdominal pain. The inability to breathe can lead to unconsciousness and death. First call 911. Then check the victim's breathing and pulse. Treatment is administration of epinephrine, which the person may have with him/her in the form of a portable autoinjector.

Hypovolemic shock happens when a person loses a lot of blood. The gums and skin under the fingernails turn blue and pale, and the skin over the body becomes cool and clammy. The eyes dilate, and pulse and breathing are rapid and shallow. Call 911 first. Check for external bleeding and apply cold compression to control it. Have the person lie down with the feet slightly elevated, and cover the person to keep them warm.

Fainting

Fainting is considered a form of shock, and it happens with the supply of blood to the brain is diminished temporarily. It commonly happens when a person stands for a long period with the knees locked, or in crowded, warm rooms where the air is stuffy and oxygen low. However, other conditions can also precipitate fainting. Prior to fainting, the person may become dizzy, pale, or nauseous. They may break out in a sweat, or describe "seeing spots." Have them lie down to prevent falling. Elevate the feet slightly and make sure they can breathe comfortably. A cool, damp cloth on the face and neck can help. Fainting might be a cause for concern in an older person, or if there is no apparent cause for it. Frequent fainting episodes might also indicate a more serious condition.

Wound Care

Bleeding is the most prominent feature of wounds needing first aid treatment. To control bleeding, first locate the source. Apply pressure at the location of the bleeding and hold it there. If possible, raise the bleeding area above the victim's heart, having the victim lie down if necessary. You can also use a tourniquet above the site of bleeding, but be careful not to block circulation entirely. Major bleeding may come from an artery or a vein. Arterial blood is bright red, and may pulse out of the wound. Venous blood is darker in color, and bleeding may be slower. Observe the victim for symptoms of shock, and give first aid for shock if needed. Note that bleeding may also be internal. Symptoms of internal bleeding include signs of shock and bruising, especially on the abdomen or trunk of the body.

The following types of wounds:

Abrasion: A scrape, caused by rubbing the skin against another surface. To treat, wash thoroughly. Be sure to remove any foreign matter from the wound.

Avulsion: A tearing off, as when a finger is cut off in machinery. Treat bleeding and proceed to an emergency room. Take the torn-off part with you if possible.

Incision: A cut. Treat bleeding and wash thoroughly. Stitches might be necessary.

Laceration: A tear. Treat bleeding and wash thoroughly. Stitches might be necessary.

Puncture: A stab. Treat bleeding and proceed to an emergency room or other medical facility. If there is an object stuck in the wound, do not attempt to remove it yourself. Note that infection risk is very high in puncture wounds.

Head Injuries

Head injuries require immediate medical attention. There may or may not be an open wound at the site of injury. Some types of head injuries include:

Skull fracture: One or more broken bones in the skull. Some symptoms might be pain, a depression in the skull at the injury site, and bleeding from the nose, mouth, or ears.

Concussion: Temporary alterations in brain functions following a blow to the head. The person may lose consciousness, or experience amnesia after the injury. Other symptoms include headache, dizziness, and vision problems.

Contusion: When a blow to the head causes bleeding, other fluid loss, and swelling inside the skull. Symptoms can include loss of consciousness, paralysis, disturbed vision, pupils dilated unequally, nausea, or amnesia. The accumulation of fluid in the skull puts pressure on the brain and can alter cognitive functioning as well.

When administering first aid, monitor breathing and consciousness, control bleeding, and watch for and treat shock.

Burns

Burns result from exposure to heat, radiation, or chemicals. Two considerations, in addition to the type of burn, are the amount of body surface that is affected and the degree of the burn. First-degree burns are superficial, affecting the skin only. Cold water or ice is appropriate initial treatments. Second degree burns cause blistering and some tissue damage below the skin. Initial first aid is soaking in cold water. If a wide area of the body is burned, watch for and treat shock. Second degree burns should receive medical attention. Third-degree burns destroy all layers of skin and burn tissue deep below the surface. Call 911, treat the victim for shock, and cover the burned area with a clean, lint-free cloth. When treating burns of any kind, do not apply lotion, ointment, or any other substance. Do not break blisters, remove tissue, or remove burnt clothing.

Professional Standards, Ethics, Business and Legal Practices

NCBTMB Code of Ethics

The sixteen principles of the NCBTMB Code of Ethics

1. Commitment to high quality of care
2. Honest representation of credentials and qualifications
3. Accurately represent the scope of massage therapy practice.
4. Refer clients to other professionals when their conditions are beyond the scope of massage treatment.
5. Only provide treatment that is to the benefit of the client.
6. Continuing education and professional development
7. Respect for all individuals
8. Obtain voluntary informed consent from clients.
9. Allow clients to refuse or end treatment when they wish.
10. Respect clients' physical privacy with appropriate draping and other techniques.
11. Maintain right to refuse services to anyone with a reasonable cause.
12. Avoid sexual relations with clients.
13. Maintain a professional relationship with clients respecting physical and emotional boundaries.
14. Refusal of gifts, benefits and the like that are intended to influence the therapist and are not of benefit to the client
15. Avoid conflicts of interest.
16. Adhere to the policies, regulations and code of the NCBTMB.

Standards of Practice

The phrase "standards of practice" refers to guiding principles by which professionals conduct themselves. Standards of practice sometimes include codes of ethics as well as regulations for certification and the like. The National Certification Board for Therapeutic Massage and Bodywork has a code of ethics that provides guidelines for conducting business, respecting clients' individuality, privacy and specific therapeutic needs, maintaining professional boundaries, and accurate representation of oneself and professional abilities. States offering licensure to massage therapists may also put forth their own standards of practice for the profession. Standards of practice are especially important in helping and healing professions, where clients may come to treatment in a vulnerable position of need, and where information exchanged between client and professional may be of a highly personal nature.

HIPAA

HIPAA stands for the Health Insurance Portability and Accountability Act. It is a measure designed to protect the privacy of a client's identifiable health information. HIPAA governs the use of and communication about patient medical records in order to ensure that such information is not used for marketing purposes or to deny other services, privileges, employment or benefits to people based on their medical conditions. Office practices that help ensure client confidentiality include not leaving medical record information lying around where it can be seen by others, not talking about client medical conditions where others can overhear, keeping patient charts in secure locations with limited access, and not releasing patient information without written consent from the patient. It is essential that practicing massage therapists stay up to date on changes in laws regarding the obtaining and using of patient medical information.

Scope of Practice

"Scope of practice" describes the range of treatments and benefits encompassed by a professional modality. Staying within one's scope of practice is an important part of maintaining professional standards and ethics. To do so means knowing exactly what massage therapy can do and what it can't, and what one is skilled in and what one isn't. Massage therapists should not diagnose medical conditions or make recommendations other than about massage treatments. They should not delve unnecessarily into clients' personal lives or give advice about non-massage related matters. Nor should they attempt to provide services that are outside the range of therapeutic massage techniques. They should not recommend medications, supplements or the like. However, remaining within scope of practice might require informing clients about what kinds of professionals do offer other services when the client comes to the therapist asking for something beyond the scope of practice. For example, the massage therapist may need to differentiate for a client what treatments are provided by massage therapists vs. chiropractors or osteopaths.

Client/Therapist Relationship

The client comes to the therapist with a need, and pays money for services. The therapist is a trusted professional in possession of specialized knowledge. These facts define the dynamics of the therapist/client relationship, one in which the client is potentially the vulnerable party. It is the responsibility to maintain and safeguard the professional boundaries of the relationship, protecting both him or herself and the client in the process. The therapist should be sensitive to any developing over-dependence on the part of the client, or a client beginning to seek emotional support outside the limitations of massage therapy. Likewise, self-observation is necessary so that if the therapist begins to feel sexual attraction, animosity, or other out-of-place feelings toward the client, he or she can refer the client to another therapist for treatment.

Business Plans

A business plan is a valuable tool to help you figure out what it will cost to establish and operate your business, and what you can hope to earn. If you are borrowing money to start the business, a detailed plan is necessary to show to potential lenders. Writing up a business plan will also help you decide what things you want to spend money on and where you can save. The business plan should include a mission statement for the business, details about the purpose and goals, a plan for marketing and advertising, a risk assessment that reviews what is happening in the field locally and more broadly, an analysis of currently available resources, and an outline of the projected policies and procedures according to which the business will operate. Goals should be very clear for the first two years of business operation, and sketched out projecting at least five years ahead.

Independent Contractor

When massage therapists work in a clinic or salon setting, they may do so either as employees or as independent contractors. Employees are paid either a salary or an hourly wage. The employer is responsible for paying a portion of an employee's social security tax, and the income tax form W-2 is filed for each employee. Taxes are withheld from an employee's pay check each pay period. Independent contractors, on the other hand, are paid for the work they do but no taxes are withheld and the income tax form 1099 is used for income reporting. The independent contractor must plan ahead to pay income and social security taxes him/herself. Massage therapists who work independently operating their own businesses will also have to assume responsibility for paying income and social security taxes, and there are tax forms appropriate for filing in this way also. If one's income is sufficiently high, it is necessary to pay quarterly estimated taxes. It is advisable to consult with a reliable accountant about the legalities, record keeping necessities and financial planning necessary to work as an independent contractor or self-employed individual.

Insurance

Massage therapists may want business and property loss insurance, disability insurance, liability insurance and malpractice insurance. They may additionally benefit from changes to car insurance, if they provide services in clients' homes or work places and use the car to get there and back. Business and property loss insurance covers loss or damage to property or equipment in the case of fire, theft and the like. Disability insurance covers situations in which the therapist becomes unable to work due to illness or injury. Liability insurance is valuable in case a client falls on the premises or otherwise is injured on site. Malpractice insurance covers the therapist if a client sues as a result of problems presumed to have been caused by the treatment services. Massage therapists who provide services to clients in the clients' homes may also wish to become bonded. Bonding is like a kind of insurance that protects professionals who work in clients' homes in case there are accusations of theft or property damage issued by the client.

Licensure

Requirements for professional licensure for massage therapists vary from state to state, and in some states licensure is not required. Sometimes there are requirements specific to cities and counties as well. In some locations, certification is required in place of or in addition to licensure. These sorts of requirements can vary not only by location, but also according to the setting in which the therapist practices, for example a medical clinic, a salon, a massage studio, an in-home business or in clients' homes. Therefore, it is essential for massage therapists to know the regulations in the geographical area and setting in which they are working. In many places, it is also necessary to have a business license or permit, and if the therapist sells products to clients, a sales tax permit is also required.

SOAP Note

SOAP is an acronym describing four components of a progress note that records information about a session with a client. The letters stand for **subjective, objective, assessment and plan.** Subjective refers to information provided by the client about his/her condition, expectations about treatment, and objectives. Objective means what the therapist observes about the client and results of tests and measurements relevant to treatment. Assessment is equivalent to diagnosis, or the therapist's summary of the client's needs, conditions and the like. Plan encompasses treatment goals and the steps projected to achieve them. SOAP is a tool to help professionals such as massage therapists chart client services and progress in an organized and professional manner, recording only what is relevant to the client's treatment.

Client Confidentiality

Confidentiality means protecting the privacy of clients, especially in regard to medical conditions, personal and financial issues, and types of services they are receiving. Health information is protected by law since the Health Insurance Portability and Accountability Act (HIPAA). However, information about a client can and should be released outside the agency providing services in several situations. These include reporting to third party payors, such as health insurance companies, cases where a client is suicidal or homicidal with intent, when records are subpoenaed by a court of law, or when abuse or neglect of a child is at issue. Therapists can discuss client cases with other professionals treating the same client for the purposes of coordination of care and treatment planning, and with supervisors as part of training and/or ongoing clinical supervision and consulting. However, they should not discuss clients in hallways, waiting rooms, public areas or anywhere else where unauthorized persons may overhear.

NCETMB Practice Test

1. Which of the following accounts for approximately 16% of the human body?

a. Integumentary system
b. Skeletal system
c Circulatory system
d. Respiratory system

2. Which of the following systems is comprised of 206 individual organs?

a. Integumentary system
b. Skeletal system
c. Circulatory system
d. Respiratory system

3. Which of the following is comprised of smooth, voluntary, and cardiac tissues?

a. Integumentary system
b. Skeletal system
c. Circulatory system
d. Muscular system

4. What three main organs make up the nervous system?

a. Brain, spinal cord, and ATP
b. Brain, skin, and nerves
c. Brain, spinal cord, and nerves
d. ATP, spinal cord, and nerves

5. Which of the following systems acts like the nervous system, but with slower reaction time and longer-lasting effects?

a. Integumentary system
b. Skeletal system.
c. Cardiovascular system
d. Endocrine system

6. Which of the following systems is a closed circuit whose main function is transportation through a network of vessels?

a. Lymphatic system
b. Skeletal system
c. Cardiovascular system
d. Endocrine system

7. Which of the following systems transports a whitish, watery fluid called lymph?

a. Lymphatic system
b. Urinary system
c. Cardiovascular system
d. Endocrine system

8. Which of the following systems produces waste in the kidney that moves to the ureters, and is stored in the urinary bladder?

a. Lymphatic system
b. Urinary system
c. Respiratory system
d. Digestive system

9. Which of the following systems functions as a means to rid the body of carbon dioxide?

a. Lymphatic system
b. Urinary system
c. Respiratory system
d. Digestive system

10. Which of the following systems include both the teeth and the pharynx?

a. Lymphatic system
b. Urinary system
c. Respiratory system
d. Digestive system

11. In the male reproductive system, what two organs make up the genitalia?

a. The gonads and the penis
b. The penis and the scrotum
c. The prostate and the vas deferens
d. The scrotum and the gonads

12. What organ is considered the female gonads?

a. Ovaries
b. Fallopian tube
c. Vagina
d. Uterine

13. Which of the following is not on the Yin meridian?

a. Moon
b. Mother
c. Acute
d. Slow

14. The liver is on the Yin meridian and is associated with what element of nature?

a. Wood
b. Fire
c. Earth
d. Metal

15. Which of the following refer to the division of the cranial and sacral segments of the spinal cord?

a. Craniosacral division
b. Sacralcranium division
c. Cranio and sacral aspects
d. Proprioception

16. Which of the following types of membrane is found in closed cavities in the body?

a. Cutaneous membranes
b. Serous membranes
c. Mucous membranes
d. Connective tissue membranes

17. What information can the width of the epiphyseal plate tell a doctor?

a. The strength of a bone
b. The estimated adult height of an individual
c. The probability of osteoporosis
d. The number of breaks a bone has had

18. What is the purpose of the synergist in movement?

a. Add support to the contracting prime mover
b. Counteract the prime mover
c. Relax as the antagonists contracts
d. Act as the main muscle in the movement

19. Neurons are named for the direction they move. What are the three types neurons found in the body?

a. Motor, Schwann, Interneurons
b. Sensory, Cranial, Interneurons
c. Sensory, Involuntary, Interneurons
d. Sensory, Motor, Interneurons

20. What is the main mechanism behind the functioning of nonsteroid hormones?

a. Negative feedback
b. Hypersecretion
c. Second messenger mechanism
d. Positive feedback

21. What is the difference between the tunica externa in an artery compared to that in a vein?

a. The tunica externa is thinner in arteries than in veins
b. The tunica externa is thicker in arteries than in veins
c. Arteries do not have a tunica externa
d. Veins do not have a tunica externa

22. What percentage of the body moves lymph in to the thoracic duct?

a. 100%
b. 75%
c. 50%
d. 25%

23. What is the main function of the respiratory membrane?

a. To line the respiratory tract with a layer of mucus
b. To act to separate air into the alveoli or the blood in the capillaries
c. To serve as a barrier to the outside air
d. To allow consistent oxygen flow into the blood stream

24. Which of the following structures begins the process of digestion?

a. Stomach
b. Small intestine
c. Teeth
d. Esophagus

25. What is manipulated in the craniosacral system during a craniosacral therapeutic session?

a. Dura mater
b. Interstitial fluid
c. Pia mater
d. Cerebrospinal fluid

26. What occurs during the process of resorption?

a. Fluid moves from the renal tubules into the blood stream
b. Fluid moves from the blood stream into the renal tubules
c. Fluid is filtered more than once
d. Elimination cannot occur and fluid is processed through the body again

27. What is the term that refers to a body standing erect with hands at the sides and palms facing forward?

a. Anatomical Position (western medicine)
b. Anatomical Position (oriental medicine)
c. Prone
d. Supine

28. The plane that goes from top to bottom, which divides the body in left and right sides directly in the middle is referred to as which of the following?

a. Sagittal
b. Frontal
c. Transverse
d. Midsagittal

29. Which of the following are located in the dorsal cavity?

a. The abdominopelvic cavity
b. The lungs
c. The thoracic cavity
d. None of the above

30. Which of the following is not a major muscle of the head?

a. Orbicularis oculi
b. Zygomaticus
c. Semimembranosus
d. Masseter

31. Which muscle has an origin at the external occipital protuberance ligamentum nuchae and an insertion at the lateral third of clavicle acromion?

a. Teres major
b. Latissimus dorsi
c. Trapezius
d. Teres minor

32. Which of the following muscles has an action of medial rotation and adduction of the humerus?

a. Supraspinatus
b. Latissimus dorsi
c. Trapezius
d. Teres minor

33. Which of the following is a depressor of the scapula?

a. Upper trapezius
b. Upper pectoralis major
c. Lower trapezius
d. Serratus anterior

34. What is occurring when a muscle contracts but no movement is produced?

a. Twitch contraction
b. Tetanic contraction
c. Isotonic contraction
d. Isometric contraction

35. What is occurring when a muscle experiences an involuntary quick movement?

a. Twitch contraction
b. Tetanic contraction
c. Isotonic contraction
d. Isometric contraction

36. What is the attachment which is on the more stationary bone?

a. Tendon
b. Origin
c. Insertion
d. Bursae

37. Which of the following connective tissues serve to anchor muscle to bone?

a. Bursae
b. Tendon
c. Ligament
d. Sarcomere

38. The iliopsoas and the adductor muscles work to move what part of the body?

a. Head and neck
b. Arms
c. Thigh
d. Feet and ankles

39. What function does the orbicularis oculi serve?

a. Bring lips together
b. Elevates corners of lips
c. Close eyes
d. Opens eyes

40. Which of the following joints are located in the skull?

a. Synarthroses
b. Amphiarthroses
c. Diarthroses
d. There are no joints in the skull

41. What is the most common type of join found in the human body?

a. Synarthroses
b. Amphiarthroses
c. Diarthroses
d. Double joints

42. A ball and socket joint can be found in what region of the body?

a. Shoulder
b. Fingers
c. Spine
d. Knee

43. Which of the following would a neurologist use to determine the specific point of damage on the spine?

a. Spinal fracture test
b. Dermatomes
c. Motor reflex test
d. Meridians

44. How many primary meridians make up the human body?

a. 10
b. 11
c. 12
d. 13

45. Which of the following secondary meridians governs all yang meridians?

a. Du Mai
b. Ren Mai
c. Chong Mai
d. Dai Mai

46. Exposure to extreme heat, surgery, and illnesses are all examples of what on the body?

a. Homeostasis
b. Disease
c. Stress
d. Heterostasis

47. Which of the following typically results from a hypersecretion of glucocorticoids?

a. Addison's disease
b. Cushing syndrome
c. Type I diabetes
d. Virilizing tumor

48. Which of the following techniques would be used by an individual participating preparing to run in a marathon in 3 days?

a. Carbohydrate loading
b. Protein loading
c. Glycogenesis
d. Antioxidant treatments

49. If a therapist was palpating the chakra of pure consciousness, where would their hand be?

a. Crown of the head
b. Between the eye brows
c. The throat
d. The chest

50. What is required for muscles to contract?

a. Myofilaments
b. Z-lines
c. ATP molecules
d. Actin

51. What type of muscle contraction is occurring is a person is sitting up straight?

a. Isotonic contraction
b. Tetanic contraction
c. Tonic contraction
d. Isometric contraction

52. What type of movement is occurring in the angle between the forearm and humorous decreases?

a. Flexion
b. Extension
c. Abduction
d. Adduction

53. Moving your arms straight out to the sides requires what type of movement?

a. Flexion
b. Extension
c. Abduction
d. Adduction

54. The downward motion of tapping your foot requires what type of movement?

a. Rotation
b. Supination
c. Dorsiflexion
d. Plantar flexion

55. Shaking your head "No" requires what type of movement?

a. Rotation
b. Supination
c. Abduction
d. Adduction

56. What must be stimulated in order to determine movement of the body?

a. Muscles
b. Chakras
c. Proprioceptors
d. Bones

57. Receptors that have some type of covering over their endings can be referred to as what?

a. Closed-end receptors
b. Encapsulated
c. Unencapsulated
d. Sheathed bulb receptors

58. In an individual with anorexia, what will the body rely on for energy once the fat stores are used up?

a. Calcium
b. Carbohydrates
c. Proteins
d. Simple sugars

59. What can occur from a deficiency of vitamin C?

a. Scurvy
b. Night blindness
c. Nerve problems
d. Pernicious anemia

60. Which of the following minerals, when deficient leads to fatigue and anemia?

a. Calcium
b. Cobalt
c. Iodine
d. Copper

61. If an individual has a deficiency in calories and protein, what disorder are they likely to have?

a. Anorexia nervosa
b. Protein deficiency
c. Pro-caloric malnutrition
d. Protein-calorie malnutrition

62. If a patient complains of pain in the left lumbar region, what organ is probably affected?

a. Descending colon
b. Stomach
c. Liver
d. Kidneys

63. Which function is responsible for maintaining equilibrium in the body?

a. Homeostasis
b. Feedback loop
c. Biorhythm
d. Brain functions

64. Which of the following has a phospholipid bilayer with proteins as its structure?

a. Ribosomes
b. Mitochondria
c. Plasma membrane
d. Lysosomes

65. If you get a paper cut on your finger, what type of tissue have you damaged?

a. Epithelial tissue
b. Connective tissue
c. Muscle tissues
d. Nervous tissue

66. Dr. Wright determined that 2-year-old Sammy will grow to be about 6-feet tall. What part of the bone did Dr. Wright look at to determine this number?

a. Diaphysis
b. Articular cartilage
c. Epiphyseal plate
d. Endosteum

67. When faced with a stressful situation, John's body began sweating. Why did this occur?

a. Activation of the parasympathetic system
b. Activation of the sympathetic system
c. Activation of the endocrine system
d. Activation of the nervous system

68. The ripple look of a toned stomach is the result of what type of muscle pattern?

a. Multipennate
b. Fusiform
c. Strap
d. Tricipital

69. Which of this client's medical situation is contraindicated for massage?

A new client comes in for a massage. She is a 35-year-old school teacher recommended by her doctor for massage. She is complaining about back and shoulder problems and state that she had shoulder surgery 8 months ago. As you read through the intake form, you also see that she is two months pregnant, has had massage in the past, and has migraine headaches. She also tells you that yesterday she fell while running and may have sprained her ankle but has not gone to the doctor.

a. Pregnancy
b. Shoulder surgery 8 months ago
c. Migraine headaches
d. Possible sprain

70. If a massage therapist is calling a doctor to talk about a client with widespread pain, how would she describe this to the doctor?

a. Pain all over
b. Fibromyalgia
c. Hypersensitivity
d. Hypo-muscle sensitivity

71. Which of the following is probably not a part of the etiology of polycystic kidney disease?

a. Cysts on the kidneys
b. Inherited
c. Mutation on PKD1 gene
d. 5% have end-stage renal disease

Questions 72-73 pertain to the following passage:

A scientist studies the pattern of diseases and finds that a disease has spread from one country to the next on a large scale. Seeing that individuals with the disease experience chest pain, coughing blood, fever, chills, and weight loss, the scientist determines it is tuberculosis. Additionally, he notices that there are a large number of individuals who had silicosis prior to contracting tuberculosis. As the scientist discusses this situation with other doctors, they decide all healthcare workers must wear masks while near and treating these patients.

72. Why must healthcare workers wear masks when caring for these patients?

a. It is an airborne illness
b. These patients emit a foul order
c. They are susceptible to other germs the healthcare workers may have
d. The air quality in the country may be very poor

73. What would a healthcare worker refer to coughing blood, fever, chills, and weight loss as?

a. Symptoms
b. Signs
c. Complaints
d. Idiopathic indications

74. Which mood-altering chemicals are released during massage that could have a profound effect on an individual with depression?

a. Serotonin
b. Estrogen
c. Adrenalin
d. Oxytocin

75. Which of the following would be most appropriate for an individual with autism?

a. No massage
b. Light, gentle strokes
c. Firm, purposeful touch
d. Hands and feet only

76. How does a general relaxation massage benefit an individual with anxiety?

a. Influences the automatic nervous system
b. Stimulates
c. Reduces hormones, causing anxiety
d. Anxiety is contraindicated

77. What must a therapist be careful of in an individual with osteoporosis?

a. Breaking a bone
b. Tearing a tendon
c. Causing emotional distress
d. Spreading the disease

78. Which of the following refers to a signed document that gives the therapist permission to work on an individual?

a. Right of refusal.
b. Informed consent
c. Contract
d. Intake questionnaire

Questions 79-82 pertain to the following passage:

> You meet a new client and provide them with all the required paperwork, including an intake questionnaire and informed consent. After they have completed and signed the paper work, you review it and ask a few questions. You find out the individual has been under a lot of stress and emotional turmoil due to the recent loss of a spouse. They tell you a friend recommends massage as a way to relax. You can understand how they are feeling because you too recently lost a loved one. After the initial interview, you begin the massage. Your client asks for a gentle massage and lets you know they are not comfortable with massage on the face and gluts.

79. What would be occurring if your client began developing feelings for you beyond the client-therapist relationship and they state you are a lot like their deceased spouse?

a. Violating legal boundaries
b. Violating personal boundaries
c. Transference
d. Countertransference

80. What would be occurring if you developed feelings for your client beyond the client-therapist relationship?

a. Violating legal boundaries
b. Violating personal boundaries
c. Transference
d. Countertransference

81. How could you as a massage therapist cross your client's personal boundaries?

a. Listen to your client throughout the massage
b. Massage their face
c. Listen and offer your assessment or opinion of their situation
d. Give them the name of a grief-counseling group

82. How could you as a massage therapist cross legal or ethical boundaries?

a. Listen to your client throughout the massage
b. Massage their face
c. Listen and offer your assessment or opinion of their situation
d. Give them the name of a grief-counseling group

83. What is one way in which different types of healthcare workers, for example, a massage therapist and a physician, can communicate?

a. Medical terminology
b. At conferences
c. Using notes to the client
d. Like normal people

84. A massage therapist that rents a room from a spa would probably file their taxes under which category?

a. Employee
b. Corporation
c. Independent contractor
d. Dependant

85. How does a massage therapist maintain an individual's privacy throughout the massage?

a. Keeping the door shut
b. Draping
c. Turning the lights on low
d. Massaging with your eyes closed

86. Why would a therapist typically not massage the armpit?

a. Endangerment site
b. The client is ticklish
c. The client does not shave
d. The client has body odor

87. Suppose a client comes for a massage and states that his back pain began about 1 year ago, in terms of level of the condition, what would this back pain be considered?

a. Acute
b. A sign
c. Chronic
d. A symptom

88. What should you do if a client comes in for a massage and is ill?

a. Send them home
b. Perform light massage
c. Refer them to a physician
d. Wear gloves

89. A massage therapist talks about their client's illnesses and conditions, using names, at the dinner table each night. What has been violated?

a. Confidentiality
b. Personal boundaries
c. Trust
d. Nothing

90. Which of the following would help a therapist document their work on a client?

a. HIPAA
b. S.O.A.P
c. ICD-10-CM
d. HPI

91. Which of the following would contraindicate lymphatic massage?

a. Congenital defect
b. Benign neoplasm
c. Malignant neoplasm
d. Chronic pain

92. A sprain with 10% fiber tear would be classified as what type of sprain?

a. Grade One
b. Grade Two
c. Grade Three
d. Grade Four

93. A traumatic injury that results in 60% muscle fiber tear and swelling would be considered which of the following?

a. First-degree strain
b. Second-degree strain
c. Third-degree strain
d. Fourth-degree strain

94. Which type of bone fracture results in the bone being completely separated?

a. Incomplete
b. Complete
c. Open
d. Fracture dislocation

95. On which of the following types of headache would you consider performing trigger point therapy?

a. Migraine
b. Cluster
c. Tension
d. Cervicogenic

96. An individual would be experiencing which of the following if they were in shock due to loss of blood?

a. Cardiogenic shock
b. Hypovolemic shock
c. Neurogenic shock
d. Anaphylactic shock

97. Which of the following is not considered an upper respiratory infection?

a. Rhinitis
b. Pharyngitis
c. Laryngitis
d. Bronchitis

98. If an individual states that they have hypernatremia, what is happening in their body?

a. Potassium imbalance
b. Sodium imbalance
c. Calcium imbalance
d. Dehydration

99. What was the earliest massage technique of the Chinese?

a. Anma
b. Ling
c. Pitta
d. Jim Shin Do

100. Which of the following is not a purpose of massage?

a. To increase cell metabolism
b. To heal illness
c. To increase ROM
d. To relieve pain

101. Breaking up adhesions using petrissage would be considered what type of effect on the body?

a. Mechanical
b. Physiological
c. Psychological
d. Pain-relieving

102. On what does lymph rely to be moved through the body?

a. Blood flow
b. Voluntary muscles
c. Involuntary muscles
d. Massage

103. What is one result of over stimulation of the nervous system to muscles?

a. Relaxation
b. Pain
c. Spasm
d. Injury

104. Which of the following is typically the first stroke to begin a massage?

a. Petrissage
b. Friction
c. Effleurage
d. Tapotement

105. Which of the following strokes can enhance fluid movement of deeper tissue?

a. Petrissage
b. Friction
c. Effleurage
d. Tapotement

106. Which of the following best describes abnormal restrictions to joint movements?

a. Reduced range of motion
b. Reduced joint movement
c. Passive joint movement
d. Active joint movement

107. Which of the following is indicated for massage?

a. Asthma
b. Abdominal aneurysm
c. Bursitis
d. Edema

108. Which of the following massage techniques uses three forms of water during the massage?

a. Aromatherapy
b. Hydrotherapy
c. Swedish massage
d. Jim Shin Do

109. Which of the following best describes an effect of hydrotherapy that affects the entire body?

a. Local effect
b. Systemic effect
c. Reflex effect
d. Thermal effect

110. Which of the following refer to the study of movement?

a. Biomechanics
b. Synergists
c. Kinesiology
d. Massage therapy

111. In Kinesiology, which of the following aspects of an assessment would include passive ROM?

a. History
b. Observation
c. Palpation
d. Specialized testing

112. According to Traditional Chinese Medicine, what element is representative of the liver?

a. Wood
b. Fire
c. Earth
d. Metal

113. Which of the following organelles are found only in the small intestine?

a. Cilia
b. Flagella
c. Microvilli
d. Centrioles

114. In terms of an active transport system, which of the following move molecules against the concentration gradient?

a. Phagocytosis
b. Pinocytosis
c. Permease System
d. Filtration

Questions 115-118 pertain to the following passage:

> Newly licensed massage therapist Amy immediately opens an office. She figures she will figure out the business aspect of owning a business as she goes. She has named her massage business "The Healing Touch" and has created signs, advertising materials, and business cards with a logo. She is on time for all massage appointments, keeps the waiting room neat and stocked with information about massage, and has her license displayed on the wall. The only records Amy keeps are the client records and she notes the date and amount paid for all massages from that client. Amy has purchased insurance including Property Damage, Bodily Injury Liability, and Malpractice insurance. Her insurance agent also suggests that she

purchase Business and Personal Property Loss and Disability insurance, but Amy declines.

115. If Amy's office undergoes a flood, leading to $1,000 in damage, why will she have to pay out-of-pocket expenses?

a. She did not purchase enough Property Damage insurance
b. She did not purchase Business & Personal Property Loss insurance
c. Floods are not covered under any insurance
d. The damage did not meet her deductible

116. A client fell in the waiting room of Amy's office, why does Amy feel secure that she is covered in this incident?

a. She has Malpractice insurance
b. She has Property Damage and Bodily Injury Liability insurance
c. She rents the office, so the landlord is responsible
d. The injury did not occur during the massage, so it is the client's responsibility

117. In the above vignette, what, concerning the business aspect, does Amy neglect to do?

a. Create a professional image
b. Purchase disability insurance
c. Develop a business plan
d. Advertise in the newspaper

118. What has Amy created by developing a logo and marketing materials?

a. A business plan
b. Professional image
c. Additional bills
d. A sound marketing plan

119. A client comes in for a massage and complains that due to a back injury, they currently rely on their family members to take care of their home. To whom might you refer this client in order to increase their quality of life and independence?

a. Chiropractor
b. Acupuncturist
c. Occupational Therapist
d. Physical Therapist

120. What are the three steps to take for a primary survey when faced with an individual who may not be breathing?

a. Airway, breathing, circulation
b. Clear the area, check breathing, check for neck injury
c. Airway, clear the area, circulation
d. Call 911, clear the area, check breathing

121. Which of the following is the most efficient standing position for a massage therapist?

a. Symmetric standing
b. Asymmetric standing
c. Knees slightly bent
d. Knees locked

122. Which of the following refers to a passive joint movement?

a. Osteokinematic movement
b. Arthrokinematic movement
c. Hinge movement
d. Joint movement

123. What is the point at which injury would occur to a joint?

a. Physiologic barrier
b. Pathologic barrier
c. Anatomic barrier
d. Range of motion

124. Which of the following describe the interconnectedness of bodywork?

a. Mind and Body
b. Mind, Body, and Spirit
c. Wholeness
d. Body and Spirit

125. For which massage therapy setting would it be most beneficial for a therapist to know and understand various dysfunctions of the body?

a. Private practice
b. Medical office
c. Spa
d. Chiropractor's office

126. On what bodily system does hydrotherapy focus?

a. Integumentary
b. Muscle
c. Autonomic nervous
d. Respiratory

127. Which of the following massage techniques could leave the client feeling fatigued and listless for up to 48 hours after the massage?

a. Hydrotherapy
b. Swedish massage
c. Lymphatic drainage
d. Reflexology

128. Which of the following is contraindicated for lymphatic drainage?

a. Simple edema
b. Low blood pressure
c. High blood pressure
d. Traveler's edema

129. What type of exercise would you recommend to a client in need of improving their breathing?

a. Dao Yin
b. Tai Ji Quan
c. Qi Gong
d. Tai Kwan Doe

130. Which of the following techniques would be used for an individual at the end stages of a terminal illness?

a. Palliative care
b. Deep tissue
c. Swedish
d. This is contraindicated

131. What is the goal of Shiatsu?

a. Relaxation
b. Balance
c. Stimulation
d. Pain relief

132. What are the most complex units in the body?

a. Cells
b. Tissues
c. Organs
d. Systems

133. Approximately what percentage of the human body is composed of oxygen, carbon, hydrogen, and nitrogen?

a. 90%
b. 93%
c. 96%
d. 100%

134. Which of the following has no nucleus?

a. White blood cells
b. Sperm cells
c. Red blood cells
d. Liver cells

135. Which of the following describes epithelia tissue that is flat and scalelike?

a. Squamous
b. Cuboidal
c. Columnar
d. Transitional

136. Which system includes oil glands?

a. Integumentary
b. Skeletal
c. Reproductive
d. Lymphatic

137. Which of the following risk factors of disease cannot be controlled by the individual?

a. Lifestyle
b. Genetic
c. Environment
d. Stress

138. Which of the following membranes are only found within closed cavities?

a. Cutaneous
b. Serous
c. Mucous
d. Connective

139. Which of the following membranes line surfaces that open to the outside of the body?

a. Cutaneous
b. Serous
c. Mucous
d. Connective

140. What is the unit within each skeletal muscle fiber?

a. Microfilaments
b. Bursae
c. Myofilaments
d. Actin

141. What are the muscles of the trunk from deep to superior?

a. Internal oblique, Transversus abdominis, Rectus abdominis, External oblique
b. External oblique, Internal oblique, Transversus abdominis, Rectus abdominis
c. Rectus abdominis, Internal oblique, Transversus abdominis, External oblique
d. Transversus abdominis, Internal oblique, Rectus abdominis, External oblique

142. Which of the following is not a part of the adductor group for the lower extremities?

a. Adductor longus
b. Gracilis
c. Iliopsoas
d. Pectineus

143. If a runner injures their biceps femoris, what will they likely be unable to do?

a. Flex their arm
b. Flex their knee
c. Flex their wrist
d. Flex their foot

144. Which of the following is not found in a long bone of an adult?

a. Diaphysis
b. Epiphysis
c. Epiphyseal plate
d. Yellow marrow

145. Which of the following is a bony landmark characterized by its large, round projection?

a. Trochanter
b. Tuberosity
c. Tubercle
d. Crest

146. Which of the following is not a function of the bones?

a. Support
b. Protection
c. Neutralizer
d. Movement

147. What type of movement is someone doing if they begin in the anatomical position and move their forearms so their palms are facing toward the back?

a. Supination
b. Pronation
c. Retraction
d. Inversion

148. What type of response is seen from muscle fibers?

a. Threshold
b. All-or-None
c. Prime
d. Antagonist

149. Which of the following is not a major section of the brain?

a. Cerebrum
b. Cerebellum
c. Diencephalon
d. Spinal cord

150. How many pairs of cranial nerves are in the human body?

a. 10
b. 11
c. 12
d. 13

151. Which sensory receptors are located in the muscles, tendons, and joints?

a. Superficial
b. Deep
c. Visceral
d. Pain

152. What tissue does the antidiuretic hormone target?

a. Kidney
b. Uterus
c. Epithelial
d. Thyroid

153. Which hormone is produced in the adrenal medulla?

a. Parathyroid hormone
b. Epinephrine
c. Aldosterone
d. Cortisol

154. Which of the following is the fluid portion of blood?

a. Interstitial
b. Intracellular
c. Plasma
d. Hemoglobin

155. What can a massage therapist do to ensure they receive all necessary information from a client?

a. Have intake forms for the clients
b. Request medical history
c. Ask the client a couple of questions
d. Assume that patients will tell them of any major conditions

156. Which of the following massage techniques includes the Vata, Pitta, and Kapha?

a. Ayurveda
b. Craniosacral
c. Esalen Massage
d. Hellerwork

157. What is characteristic of the Lomi-Lomi technique?

a. Rapid movement
b. Short strokes
c. Broad strokes
d. The use of scented oils

158. In which of the following cases would conduction occur?

a. Stone massage
b. Sauna
c. Using an ultrasound
d. Warming the massage room

159. What hydrotherapy technique may be used to treat the pelvic region only?

a. Whirlpool bath
b. Sitz bath
c. Ice packs
d. Alcohol rub

160. What is one of the most important skills a massage therapist must have for interviewing clients and general communication?

a. Remembering everything the clients says
b. Reassuring the client massage will help
c. Active listening
d. Writing things down

Answer Key and Explanations

1. A: The Integumentary system, also known as the skin, accounts for approximately 16% of the human body. In the average adult, the skin alone weighs approximately 20 pounds. While this system is also referred to as the skin, it is important to note that the hair, nails, and sweat and oil glands are also included in this system. Within this system, particularly in the skin, lie sense organs that allow a person to feel temperature, pain, and pressure. This main function of the Integumentary system is to provide protection to the other organs and tissues in the body, as well as to serve as temperature regulator and a means to synthesize various chemicals.

2. B: The Skeletal system is composed of 206 bones that provide the structure and support for the human body. In addition to the bones, within this system are tissue, cartilage, and ligaments that provide the connections and support for the bones themselves. Within the skeletal system, there are two main parts, which include the axial skeleton and the appendicular skeleton. The Axial skeleton includes the bones of the skull, the ribs, and the neck and spine. The appendicular skeleton includes the bones in the shoulder, arm and hands, pelvis, legs, and feet. These two divisions of the skeletal system are attached at the pectoral girdle, the group including the scapula and the clavicle.

3. D: The Muscular system is made up of three different muscle types including the smooth muscles, cardiac muscles, and voluntary muscles. The smooth muscles also referred to as involuntary muscles can be found in the colon, stomach, and eyes. These muscles work constantly and do not require conscious thought to perform. Voluntary muscles also referred to as skeletal muscles, take conscious effort in order to be put into action. These muscles are found on the skeleton and assist in movement. Cardiac muscles are found in the heart and are involuntary.

4. C: The nervous system includes the brain, spinal cord, and the nerves. This system serves a number of functions including communication from the brain to the body, control, and integration. All processes completed by the nervous system are completed through nerve impulses that move quickly through the body to the brain, relaying various messages. These messages will depend on which stimuli are present. For example, if you touch something hot, the nerves in your hand will relay a message to the brain based on the stimuli, the brain will process and response by sending nerve impulses back to the hand, telling the hand that it is hot.

5. D: The Endocrine system functions much like the nervous system in that it communicates, integrates, and controls. The way this system accomplishes these functions is by secreting hormones throughout the body through a series of ducts and glands. Some of the main activities the endocrine system controls and regulates include growth, metabolism, reproduction, etc. Glands within this system are ductless and are located throughout the body. For examples, in the brain are the pituitary gland and the hypothalamus, in the neck are the thyroid and the parathyroid glands, the thymus gland in the thoracic cavity, and just below in the abdominal cavity are the adrenal glands and the pancreas.

6. C: The Cardiovascular system is made up of the heart, arteries, veins, and capillaries that transport nutrients, oxygen, carbon dioxide, and waste through the blood to all sections of the body. This closed-circuit system also serves to regulate body temperature and some specialized cells of the cardiovascular system assist with the immune system. Also called the circulatory system, blood travels through the heart, leaving it by way of arteries and continues through the arterioles, capillaries, venules, and veins. The blood then returns to the heart through veins. In addition to this systemic circulation, pulmonary circulation is the process for transporting blood to the lungs;

hepatic portal circulation transports blood through the liver, and fetal circulation transports blood to and from a fetus.

7. A: The Lymphatic system transports lymph and is composed of the lymph nodes, lymphatic vessels, and other lymphatic organs such as the tonsils, spleen, and the thymus gland. Lymph contains various fatty molecules, proteins, and lymphocytes. It must be noted that there are no red blood cells within the Lymphatic system. While the lymph is transported through its own lymphatic vessels, this material will eventually travel through ducts in to the main blood stream. Two common areas in the body where lymph can be found include the armpit and the groin, were there are large collections of lymph nodes.

8. B: The Urinary system is composed of the kidneys, ureters, the bladder, and the urethra. Within this system, it is the kidney's role to clear the blood that is transported into this organ. This blood, before it is cleaned, contains waste from metabolized food. Once waste, or urine, is produced in the kidneys, it travels out of this organ in to the ureters and is stored in the bladder. As the urine leaves the body it will flow from the bladder through the urethra. Other organs that serve to rid the body of waste include the intestines, skin, and lungs.

9. C: The Respiratory system rids the body of carbon dioxide. Within the system are the nose, pharynx, larynx, trachea, bronchi, and the lungs. This system can be further broken down in to the upper respiratory system (nose, pharynx, and larynx) and the lower respiratory system (trachea, bronchi, and the lungs). Air enters the respiratory system through the nose travels through the pharynx in to the larynx to the trachea and the bronchi into the lungs, into alveoli. Alveoli are small, thin sacs where oxygen is exchanged for carbon dioxide and the carbon dioxide leaves the body. In cold climates, the air is warmed in the upper respiratory system.

10. D: The Digestive or gastrointestinal system included the teeth and the pharynx. Additionally, this system includes the mouth, esophagus, stomach, small intestine, large intestine, rectum, anal canal, salivary glands, tongue, live, gallbladder, pancreas and the appendix. This system is divided in to two groups, which include primary organs (mouth, esophagus, pharynx, stomach, small intestine, large intestine, rectum, anal canal) and accessory organs (teeth, salivary glands, tongue, liver, gallbladder, pancreas, and the appendix). As food passes through the digestive tract, important nutrients will be absorbed by the body and the remaining will exit the body as waste product.

11. B: The penis and the scrotum make up the male genitalia in the male reproductive system. Within this system, the genitalia are considered supporting organs. Additionally, in the male reproductive system the gonads, or testes, are responsible for sperm production. The vas deferens and the prostate also act as accessory organs in the process of reproduction. During reproduction, the sperm travels from the testes through the vas deferens and other genital ducts through the urethra and out of the body. In this process, the prostate is responsible for producing nutrient-filled fluid that assists in reproduction.

12. A: Within the female reproductive system, the ovaries are the female gonads. Eggs are produced in the ovaries and travel through the fallopian tubes and will attach to the wall of the uterus if fertilized. Other organs in the female reproductive system include the vagina, vulva, and the mammary glands. The vagina is a tube approximately 10-cm long and is composed of involuntary muscle. It is located in between the balder and the rectum in the pelvic cavity. The vagina is also referred to as the birth canal. The vulva is the external female genitalia. Finally the mammary glands, located in the breast, are also considered external sex organs.

13. C: Acute is not on the Yin meridian. The Yin and Yang meridians in oriental medicine refer to various parts of the body as well as various functions. The following elements are on the Yin meridian: moon, earth, woman, mother, water, nothing, cold, matter, interior, interior, anterior, medial, structure, quiet, slow, chronic, upward, and negative. The following elements are on the Yang meridian: sun, heaven, man, father, fire, everything, hot, energy, superior, exterior, posterior, lateral, functioning, restless, rapid, acute, downward, and positive. The Yin and Yang are opposites, as are their associated elements.

14. A: The liver is associated with the element of wood. According to oriental medicine, the liver serves to regulate smoothness and makes sure the chi flow is going in the proper direction. As each organ has a pair, the liver's Yang pair is the gall bladder, which regulates courage and controls the individual's intuition in terms of decision-making. If these organs are in dis-ease they will be indicated by dry eyes and nails and blurry vision. This time for the liver according to the body clock is from 1:00 am to 3:00 am. Finally, the liver begins at LV1 (dorsal aspect of the big toe) and ends LV14 (mammillary line, 6th intercostal space).

15. A: The Craniosacral division is the nerves of the parasympathetic division that lead off from the cranial and the sacral segments of the spinal cord. This system results in an opposite response to the sympathetic systems, and includes the contraction of the pupils and the return to a normal heart rate. In addition to these effects, the craniosacral system as a whole has an impulse called the craniosacral impulse. This impulse can be palpated through slow and steady body work. The impulse is the rhythm of the individual's body and will vary from person to person.

16. B: Serous membranes are found in the closed cavities of the body. This type of membrane is classified as an epithelial membrane and is made up of two layers. This top layer is the squamous epithelium and the bottom layer is connective tissues called the basement membrane. Additionally, these membranes are named according to where in the body they are located and what they cover, and more specifically, when covering the wall of a cavity it is termed a parietal portion and when covering an organ this membrane is termed the visceral portion. Serous membranes within the thoracic cavity are referred to as pleura, and those within the abdominal cavity are referred to at peritoneum. Therefore, the serous membrane that covers the wall of the abdominal cavity is called the parietal peritoneum, covering the organs within the abdominal cavity referred to as the visceral peritoneum. Those covering the lining of the thoracic cavity are referred to as the parietal pleura, whereas those covering the organs within the thoracic cavity are called visceral pleura.

17. B: The width of the epiphyseal plate can provide information for an estimate of the adult height of an individual. The epiphyseal plate is located between the epiphyses and the diaphysis within bone and as children, this is a cartilage substance. This estimate may be made when the individual is a child, prior to ossification. A common technique for this estimation is obtaining an x-ray of a child's bones, often the wrist, and determining if and how much of the epiphyseal plate is cartilage. As the child grows, this plate will completely transform into bone, at which point the individual will stop growing.

18. A: As a muscle moves, the synergist provides support to the prime mover. Both the synergist and the prime mover muscles contract while the antagonist muscles relax. Therefore, the movement of pulling your forearm up requires your biceps brachii to be the prime movers and the bicep brachialis serve as the synergists. The triceps are the antagonist of the movement because they are required to relax in order to stretch out. As the forearm is moved back down in a straight position, the role of these muscles is reversed and the triceps becomes the prime mover and the biceps brachii the antagonist.

19. D: Sensory neurons provide information to the brain from various parts of the body. This type of neuron is also referred to as afferent neurons. Motor neurons, also referred to as efferent neurons, send signals and information from the brain to either muscle or glandular epithelial tissue. These neurons send signals that tell the various parts of the body what to do. Interneurons act as connecting neurons as they send information from the motor neurons to the sensory neurons. Together, these three types of neurons create a loop-type system of information transfer. As an example of this process, if an individual touches something hot, that information will be sent up to the brain through the sensory neurons; once the brain processes the information, it is sent back through motor neurons. The interneurons come into play when information must be passed from the sensory to the motor neurons and vice versa.

20. C: The second messenger mechanism is the main mechanism of functioning for nonsteroid hormones. For this process, a first messenger is required; commonly a protein hormone which will attach to a specific receptor site on the cell membrane. Once the connection between the protein hormone and the cell receptor site has been accomplished, chemical reaction occurs and activates the second messengers, which are in the cell. Once the second messengers are activated, then the hormone can carry out its specific function. This process is a form of communication between the hormones and the cells. A common example of this process can be demonstrated by the hormone adenosine monophosphate, which is a second messenger that provides the cell with necessary information for activity.

21. A: The tunica externa is the outermost layer of both an artery and a vein, and is thinner in arteries. This layer is composted of connective tissue, and its primary function is that of support and reinforcement of the artery or vein to prevent bursting under the pressure of blood flow. In addition to this layer, arteries and veins also have a tunica media, responsible for the regulation of blood pressure, and tunica intima, a smooth film lining arteries and veins that prevents unintentional blood clotting. Unique to veins are the semilunar valves located within the tunica intima. These valves prevent backflow of blood as it travels back to the heart.

22. B: Approximately 75% of the body dumps its lymph into the thoracic duct. The thoracic duct is located on the left subclavian vein and is the largest lymphatic vessel in the body. Lymph for all parts of the body except the upper right extremity flows through the thoracic duct. In addition to the thoracic duct, the right lymphatic duct is located on the right subclavian vein. Lymph from the right sides of the head, neck, chest, and right arm enter into the right lymphatic duct. All lymph flows in one direction and eventually enters back into the blood stream to be discarded as waste. Additionally, a structure in the abdomen, called the cistern chili, acts as a storage area for lymph traveling toward the thoracic duct.

23. B: The respiratory membrane acts to separate air into the alveoli, or the blood in the capillaries. This membrane can be found lining the wall of the alveoli, which are small sacs that fill with air located at the end of the bronchioles. The respiratory membrane consists of various layers including the alveolar wall, interstitial fluid, and the pulmonary capillary wall. The alveolar wall is comprised of epithelial cells, while the pulmonary capillary wall is made up of endothelial cells. The process of oxygen and carbon dioxide travelling across the respiratory membrane is diffusion.

24. C: Digestion begins in the mouth with the teeth. The teeth serve digestion by breaking food down for further processing. While the mouth is considered a main organ within the digestive system, the teeth are accessory organs. The tongue, also an accessory organ, assists the teeth in this initial breakdown of food. From the mouth, food will travel down the pharynx to the esophagus, then to the stomach, the small intestine, the large intestine, the rectum, and finally the anal canal. As the food moves through this system, various chemical reactions occur and food is metabolized as essential nutrients are removed and distributed or stored in the body as needed.

25. D: Cerebrospinal fluid is manipulated during a craniosacral therapeutic session. This fluid can be found between the dura mater, the arachnoid membrane, and the pia mater. These three layers of membrane make up the meningeal system. More specifically, the dura mater is the outermost membrane and functions as waterproof protection. The arachnoid membrane is the middle layer, and provides the necessary lubrication for the outer- and innermost membranes of this system to easily glide. Finally, the pia mater is the innermost membrane that lines the brain and spinal cord. Because the cerebrospinal fluid serves as lubrication between these membrane layers, if this fluid is not flowing freely through the craniosacral system, then pain may result.

26. A: With the process of resorption, fluid moves from the renal tubules into the blood stream. Common substances that undergo the process of resorption include water, proteins, sodium, and other essential nutrients. Resorption begins at the proximal convoluted tubules through the loop of Henle, through the distal convoluted tubules and into the collecting tubules. Resorption occurs through osmosis, and nearly 99% of water is resorbed on a daily basis. Additionally, one nutrient, glucose, is also resorbed. The body's inability to resorb glucose results in a condition referred to as glycosuria, or glucose in the urine, which is a sign of diabetes mellitus.

27. A: The Anatomical Position, according to western medicine, is achieved when the body standing erect with hands at the sides and palms facing forward. In addition, the head and feet also face forward. This universal position allows communication between professionals in the healthcare industry. Using the anatomical position as a reference point, we are able to discuss and locate various parts of the body. In terms of referencing the body using this position, anatomical directions include superior (toward the head) and inferior (away from the head); anterior (front) and posterior (back); medial (toward the midline) and lateral (toward the side); proximal (toward the trunk) and distal (away from the trunk); and superficial (near the surface) and deep (away from the surface).

28. D: The midsagittal is the plane that goes from top to bottom, which divides the body in left and right sides directly in the middle. This should not be confused with the sagittal plane, which divides the body in left and right sides but does not do so directly down the middle of the body or organ. Other planes that are used to determine and discuss a specific location of the body include frontal, running side to side and dividing the body into front and back, and transverse, running horizontally, dividing the body into top and bottom.

29. D: None of the above. The abdominopelvic cavity and the thoracic cavity are divisions of the ventral cavity. The lungs are contained within the thoracic cavity. The dorsal cavity consists of the cranial cavity and spinal canal.

30. C: The semimembranosus is not a major muscle of the head, but is in fact a muscle of the hamstring group, with an insertion at the tibia and origin at the ischium and functions to flex the knee. The Orbicularis oculi is located above the eye, with an insertion and origin at the maxilla and functions to closes the eye. The Zygomaticus is located at the cheek with an insertion at the angle of the mouth and upper lip and an origin at the Zygomatic arch and functions to elevate the corners of the mouth. Finally, the Masseter is located at the jaw with an insertion at the mandible and an origin at the Zygomatic arch and functions to close the mouth.

31. C: The trapezius has an origin at the external occipital protuberance ligamentum nuchae and an insertion at the lateral third of clavicle acromion. The trapezius also has an origin at the C7-T12 spinous process and two additional insertions at the spine of the scapula and the root of the spine of the scapula. The trapezius is a triangular shaped muscle and is the most superficial muscle in the back. The action of the trapezius is elevation and upward rotation of the scapula, and retraction of the scapula. This muscle lies superior to the latissimus dorsi, and the teres major and minor.

32. B: The latissimus dorsi has an action of medial rotation and adduction of the humerus. This muscle also has an origin at the thoracolumbar aponeurosis, the lower six thoracic spinous processes, the iliac crest and the sacrum, the lower 4 ribs, and the inferior angle of the scapula. The insertion of the latissimus dorsi is at the bicipital groove of the humerus. This muscle is the widest muscle in the back and is very useful for activities that require a lot of power such as swimming. In addition to the action of rotation, the latissimus dorsi is responsible for extension.

33. C: The lower trapezius is a depressor of the scapula.

34. D: An isometric contraction occurs when a muscle contracts but no movement is produced. Isometric is a Greek word meaning "equal measure." As it pertains to muscle movement and contraction, if a muscle shortens, then it will move. However, in this type of muscle contraction the length in the relaxed state is the same, or equal to the length of the muscle in the contracted state. What is occurring within the muscle during an isometric contraction is that the muscle tension increases. This type of contraction can be accomplished by pushing or pulling on a stationary object.

35. A: A twitch contraction is an involuntary, quick movement. This type of muscle contraction typically occurs in response to a stimulus; for example, a fly landing on your arm or touching something too hot or too cold. Research on muscle contractions such as twitches has been able to isolate individual muscles and cause these individual muscle fibers to twitch. However, in real-life movements, a twitch will not occur on an isolated muscle fiber due to the all-or-none response. This muscle response is one in which either all the fibers of a muscle move, or none of them move.

36. B: The origin is the muscle attachment on the more stationary bone. Every muscle will have an origin and there are a number of muscles that have more than one origin. The tendons, on the other hand, are tissue that connects the muscle to the bone. Tendons will be found at both the insertion and the origin of the muscle. The insertion is the part of the muscle that is attached on the more movable part. Finally the bursae are sacs filled with fluid located between the tendon and the bone. These fluid-filled sacs help with movement by providing a lubricant called the synovial fluid.

37. B: Tendons anchor the muscle to the bone. Tendons are made up of dense connective tissue so that the muscle firmly attaches to bone. Tendons are further protected by tendon sheaths. These tendon sheaths are lined with a synovial membrane that provides lubrication to the tendon in order to allow for easy movement. The bursae can be found between some tendons and the bone and serve to provide lubrication to decrease friction between the tendon and bone. Without the tendon sheaths and the bursae, movement would be painful and very difficult, because the tendons would not be able to easily move, and the friction between the bone and the tendon would result in tearing.

38. C: The iliopsoas and the adductor muscles serve to move the lower extremities. Specifically, the iliopsoas has an origin at the ilium and vertebrae and an insertion at the femur. This muscle flexes the thigh and the trunk of the body. Other muscles that move the thigh or the trunk of the body include the sartorius (flexes thigh and rotates legs) and the gluteus maximus (extends thigh). The adductor muscles are a group that includes the adductor longus, gracilis, and the pectineus, all of which adduct the thigh. All three adductor muscles have an origin at the pubis, while the adductor longus and pectineus have an insertion at the femur and the gracilis has an insertion at the tibia.

39. C: The orbicularis oculi closes the eyes. This muscle has an origin and insertion at the maxilla and the frontal bone, and therefore circles the eye. Another muscle that moves the eyes is the frontal muscle with an origin at the occipital bone and insertion at the eyebrow, this muscle raises the eyebrows. The muscles that move the eyes are important for facial expressions. While these muscles move the eye brows and eye lids, there are a number of muscles in the skull that move the eyeball itself. These include the medial, lateral, superior, and inferior rectus muscles, and the superior and inferior oblique muscles.

40. A: The skull contains synarthroses joints, also referred to as suture because of the suture-like appearance. In newborns these joints are not fully formed, resulting in the soft spot on the top of the head which is fibrous tissue. As the child grows, the bones close. These joints are immobile because connective tissue has grown between the bones. While synarthroses joints are often discussed in terms of having no movement, those in the skull do have slight movement caused by the ebb and flow of spinocranial fluid. In craniosacral therapy, the bones in the skull are palpated and the therapist can feel the movement of these bones.

41. C: Diarthrosis joints are the most common type of joint in the human body. These joints move freely. All diarthrosis joints have three common structures, which include the joint capsule, joint cavity, and cartilage covering the ends of the two adjoining bones. These structures are made up of connective tissues and synovial membranes that allow the joint to move in one or more directions. The type of movement a diarthrosis joint has will depend on its location within the body and the specific joint type. Joint types include ball and socket, hinge, pivot, saddle, gliding, and condyloid.

42. A: The joint in the shoulder is a ball and socket joint. This type of joint allows full movement of the shoulder which includes side to side, up and down, and in a circular motion. With ball and socket joints, the end of one bone is shaped like a ball and the end of the other bones is a concave, cup-like shape. These two bones fit snuggly together with a synovial membrane separating them to reduce friction and allow easy movement. When a joint is "popped out of socket" this is referring to this ball and socket joint, when the ball end comes out of the socket end.

43. B: Neurologists use dermatomes to determine the exact location of a spinal injury. Dermatomes refer to specific locations on the skin surface that are connected to only one nerve. Looking at a dermatome map of the body, one can see that the skin surface is divided into 5 segments, or dermatomes; cervical, thoracic, lumbar, sacral, and coccygeal. Within each of these segments are further divisions or layers that connect to a specific nerve. More specifically, there are 8 cervical, 12 thoracic, 5 lumbar, 5 sacral, and one coccygeal nerve; therefore each segment has the corresponding subdivisions.

44. C: There are 12 primary meridians in the human body including the lung, colon, stomach, spleen, heart, intestine, triple warmer, pericardium, urinary bladder, kidney, gallbladder, and liver meridians. Each point of these meridians corresponds to a location, function, and time in the body, and all primary meridians correspond to an internal organ. In oriental medicine, meridians carry the flow of Qi to all parts of the body. The flow of Qi is as follows: note the time in parentheses refers to the time of activity for that organ: lungs (3:00 am-5:00 am), large intestine (5:00 am-7:00 am), stomach (7:00 am-9:00 am), spleen (9:00 am-11:00 am), heart (11:00 am-1:00 pm), small intestine (1:00 pm-3:00 pm), urinary bladder (3:00 pm-5:00 pm), kidney (5:00 pm-7:00 pm), pericardium (7:00 pm-9:00 pm), triple warmer (9:00 pm-11:00 pm), gallbladder (11:00 pm-1:00 am), and liver (1:00 am-3:00 am).

45. A: The Du Mai, also referred to as the Governing Vessel, governs all Yang channels. This meridian begins at the anus (REN-1) and runs up the spine, over the skull, and ends at the inside of the upper lip (DU-28). While this is the main path of the governing vessel, the Du Mai also has three other pathways along the body: (1) beginning in the lower abdomen down through the tip of the coccyx and up the spine ending at the kidneys; (2) beginning in the lower abdomen traveling up to the forehead; and (3) beginning in the lower abdomen, traveling across the umbilicus, and moving up toward the heart. When there is weakness in this meridian, an individual may experience symptoms of stiffness, back pain, and headache.

46. C: Stress is the condition in which the body is not in balance. Stressors on the body can range and include physical or mental stimuli. During stress glucocorticoid production and release is increased by the adrenal cortex. This process is the first step in the stress response. Once glucocorticoid concentrations are elevated in the body, there is an increase in the amount of fats and proteins that are metabolized atrophy in the thymus, and the inflammatory response becomes inhibited. From here other stress responses are put into action until the body once again reaches homeostasis, or balance.

47. B: Cushing syndrome typically results from a hypersecretion of glucocorticoids. This syndrome is characterized by physical abnormalities such as moon-face and buffalo hump. These abnormalities are cause because of an abnormal redistribution of fat causing the face or upper back, respectively to be larger and more rounded than normal. Another common symptom of this syndrome is an increased production of testosterone leading to the appearance of male secondary sexual characteristics. This syndrome is more common in women and individuals with Cushing have higher than normal blood sugar levels and frequent infections. The physical abnormalities of this syndrome can be corrected with surgery.

48. A: Carbohydrate loading would be the most beneficial nutritional practice or technique for an individual preparing for a marathon. Carbohydrate loading is the intake of a large amount of carbohydrates for storage in the body, specifically, in skeletal muscle fibers. When athletes consume a high carbohydrate diet, they are able to store up to two times as many carbohydrates as normal. This additional energy will allow them to sustain physical activity for a longer period. As energy is needed, the body takes the stored carbohydrates and processes them through glucose catabolism, which has three stages: (1) glycolysis; (2) citric acid cycle; and (3) electron transfer system.

49. A: The crown of the head is the location of the chakra of pure consciousness, also known as the Crown Chakra, or Sahasrara. Chakras are forces of energy rotating in the body. This chakra can be compared to the pituitary gland, hypothalamus, and the thalamus. The Crown Chakra serves to communicate with the body and connects the central nervous system with the hypothalamus and thalamus. This chakra is indicated with the color violet and the lotus flower. Other components of the Crown Chakra include its connection of inner wisdom, death, universal consciousness, and meditation.

50. C: Muscle contraction requires energy or ATP molecules. With a muscle contraction, all parts of the muscle are involved, otherwise known as an all-or-nothing response. Specifically, the muscle is composed of fibers with thick and thin myofilaments that produce proteins, myosin and actin, respectively, upon contraction. The action of a contracting muscle can be observed by looking at the sarcomeres. As the muscle contrasts, the distance between the z-lines of the sarcomeres shortens, whereas when the muscle relaxes, the distance increases. Thick and thin myofilaments slide toward each other, overlapping during muscle contraction. This is also referred to as the sliding filament model.

51. C: In a tonic contraction, there is no muscle movement. However, the muscles do serve to support the body. A tonic contraction will occur anytime an individual is in an upright position. Another way to describe this type of contraction is posture. Individuals with good posture have strong muscles that are also properly aligned with other parts of the body; the opposite is true for individuals with poor posture. The muscles specifically involved in maintaining posture are back and neck muscles, because gravity tends to pull the head and trunk of the body down.

52. A: Flexion occurs when there is a decrease in the angle between two bones. In addition to the decrease in the angle, during flexion, there is a decrease in the length of the prime mover and an increase in the length of the antagonist associated with the bones. In this example, when the angle between the forearm and the humorous decreases, the length of the bicep decreases while the triceps increase in length. Similar to flexing the arm, one can also flex the leg in which one would bend the leg back at the knee, shortening the hamstring muscle group and lengthening the quadriceps.

53. C: Abduction is a movement away from the midline. By moving your arms straight out to the sides and away from the midline, you are abducting your arms. Muscles involved in this type of movement include the deltoid as the prime mover and rotator cuff muscles as the synergists. In order for abduction to occur, the deltoid must contract. Additionally, the glenohumeral joint is also involved. The opposite movement to abduction is adduction. Adduction is the movement toward the midline. When you bring your arms back down to your body, adduction occurs.

54. D: Plantar flexion results in the toes pointing downward. Plantar flexion is also required to move into a position where you are standing on your toes. This movement will increase the degree of the angle between the top of the foot and the ankle. The primary muscles involved in plantar flexion include the gastrocnemius, soleus, plantaris, flexor hallucis longus, flexor digitorum longus, and the tibialis posterior. The lateral muscles involved in this movement include the peroneus longus and peroneus brevis. The opposite movement is dorsiflexion, which results in the toes pointing upward and decreased the degree of the angle between the top of the foot and the ankle.

55. A: Rotation is the movement that occurs when shaking your head "no." This movement occurs around a longitudinal axis. The main joint type in the neck that allows this movement is a condyloid joint. Other types of rotation include internal rotation, also referred to as media rotation. Internal rotation is a rotation toward the midline. For example, you can rotate your shoulder or hip toward your midline. External rotation, or lateral rotation, is the movement of rotation away from the midline. Rotating your hip out so your toes point away from the midline is an example of external rotation.

56. C: Proprioceptors are receptors found between tendons and muscles as well as deep within the skeleton that provide the brain with information about body position or movement. These receptors are enclosed. When there is trauma to a proprioceptor, it could result in permanent damage, leading to the loss of feeling of the muscles. Two important proprioceptors include the Golgi tendons and muscle spindles. Golgi tendons are located at the junction of tendons and muscles and detect tension the muscle. Muscle spindles located in all skeletal muscles detect the length of a muscle.

57. B: Receptors are often distinguished by whether or not they are encapsulated (covered) or unencapsulated (free or naked). There are six main encapsulated receptors. Meissner's corpuscles located on the skin, fingertips, and lips and detect very fine touches and low frequency vibrations. Ruffini's corpuscles are also located at the dermal layer of the skin and the subcutaneous tissues of the fingers and detect both touch and pressure. The Pacinian corpuscles are located at various levels of tissues at joints, the mammary glands, and external genitalia and detect pressure and high frequency vibrations. Krause's end-bulbs are located in the skin, lips, eyelids, and external genitalia and detect touch and cold. Golgi tendons and muscle spindles, located in skeletal muscles detect muscle tension and length.

58. C: Anorexia is an illness in which the individual starves themselves. In these cases the body will compensate for the lack of nutrients and use up all available resources. This begins with the use of all stored fat throughout the body. Following this, the body will begin to use up its protein stores in order to provide itself with energy. During this process, the protein molecules will go through catabolism and the amino acids making up these proteins will be broken down and converted into glucose which then begins the citric acid cycle. Because the body needs proteins for survival, when the body uses these proteins solely for energy, death may occur.

59. A: An individual with a vitamin C deficiency may develop scurvy. Scurvy is characterized by the inability to make and maintain collagen fibers which is necessary for connective tissues. Common physical symptoms of scurvy include skin spots, spongy gums, and bleeding. Prior to modern day technologies and knowledge about the importance of vitamins, this disease was very common among sailors who may not have had efficient access to the fruits and vegetables that provide vitamin C. While if untreated, scurvy can be fatal, individuals with this disease can make full recoveries with the intake of vitamin C.

60. D: Copper is an essential mineral. Individuals deficient in copper may experience fatigue and anemia. Adequate amounts of copper can be found in seafood, organ meats, and legumes. Copper's primary function in the body with regard to metabolism is to extract energy from the citric acid cycle of catabolism as well as during the production of blood. In addition to these functions, copper also serves to provide the blood with oxygen and maintain healthy hair color. While copper can be obtained from various foods, the body is also able to absorb copper through the skin and many individuals have found wearing copper jewelry, particularly bracelets, beneficial for ailments such as arthritis.

61. D: Protein-calorie malnutrition, also referred to as PCM, is a deficiency in calories and protein in particular. This disorder is typically the result of an individual eating less; however, it can also occur if the body begins to use up more nutrients than normal. This type of malnutrition is often seen in mild form during most illnesses. More extreme cases of this type of malnutrition can be seen in various disorders. For example, those disorders that cause a reduced nutrient intake include: anorexia, self-induced starvation; dysphagia, inability or difficulty swallowing; gastrointestinal obstructions; and nausea. Disorders that result in the loss of nutrients include diarrhea; glycosuria, glucose in the urine; and hemorrhage. Finally, those that cause the body to use more nutrients than normal include burns, fever, and infection.

62. A: The descending colon is likely to be affected when a patient complains of pain in the left lumbar region. The abdominopelvic cavity is divided in to four regions: Right upper, Left upper, Right lower, and Left lower. Within these regions the abdominopelvic cavity is further divided in to nine sections. By dividing this cavity into sections, healthcare workers are also to communicate clearly about a patient. With regard to the nine sections, these include the right hypochondriac region, epigastric region, left hypochondriac region, Right lumbar region, umbilical region, left lumbar region, Right iliac region, hypogastric region, and the left iliac region.

63. B: The feedback loop is the primary function that maintains homeostasis in the human body. This feedback loop detects when the body is unbalanced and triggers the appropriate mechanisms to bring it back into balance, much like the principles of input and output seen in engineering.

Essentially, the nerve endings are the sensors that send messages to the brain, or control center, where the information is processed and acted upon. For example, on a cold day, the skin senses the cold temperature, sends this information to the brain; and the brain tells the muscles (effectors) to shiver, thus bringing the body temperature up. When the body temperature is at the appropriate level, the shivering will stop.

64. C: The plasma membrane's structure is a phospholipid bilayer with proteins. This part of the cell serves as a barrier and protects the cell. On the outer surface of this membrane, protein and carbohydrates have the function of markers to differentiate cells from one another. These components also serve to identify various receptor cells for hormones that will only act on specific cells. The plasma membrane is approximately seven nanometers thick and in addition to protecting the cell, this membrane keeps the cell together with the layers of phospholipid as well as cholesterol that helps stabilize the phospholipids.

65. A: A paper cut will damage the epithelial tissue. Epithelial tissue covers the outside of the body and is a protective barrier. This type of tissue also covers the cavities within the body. The cells of epithelial tissues are packed closely together and cell division is rapid. There are three types of epithelial tissue, cutaneous membrane, serous membrane, and mucous membrane. Cutaneous membranes are the most visible and most abundant in the body, as this type of tissue makes up the skin. Serous membranes are located within closed cavities and have two layers, an epithelial sheet and a layer of simple squamous epithelium. Finally, the mucous membranes are located in cavities that open to the exterior, for example, in the respiratory organs.

66. C: The epiphyseal plate will be the part of the bone that a doctor will look at to determine the adult height of an individual. This structure is made of cartilage and is located between the epiphysis and the diaphysis of the long bone. As the child grows, the epiphyseal plate will begin to harden and when all of the cartilage is harden into bone, growth stops. Once growth stops, what is left is the epiphyseal line marking the point where the epiphysis and the diaphysis have joined. Height can be determined by the thickness of the cartilage, typically by x-raying the wrist.

67. B: The sympathetic system is responsible for responding in emergency situations. This system is a part of the larger autonomic nervous system and is also referred to as the thoracolumbar division. This is often referred to as the fight or flight response. During these situations the sympathetic system will cause a number of other systems or responses to go at the same time. This increased activation of responses allows the body the energy necessary to deal with the stressful situation. Examples of increased responses include sweating, increased heart rate, and secretion of epinephrine, a hormone of the adrenal medulla that reinforces the effects of norepinephrine.

68. C: The muscle pattern that causes the rippled look of a toned stomach is called strap. With this pattern the muscle fibers are aligned and parallel. Other muscle patterns are pinnate, bipennate, multipennate, and triangular, in which fibers are in a diagonal pattern. A fusiform pattern is one in which the fibers are parallel in the belly of the muscle. Spiral and tricipital fibers are twisted and have three muscle bellies, respectively. These patterns are clearly visible and will vary depending on the muscle and its function. For example, the deltoids have a multipennate pattern; the trapezius has a triangular pattern; and the latissimus dorsi has a spiral pattern.

69. D: The possible sprain is contraindicated for massage until a doctor has examined the injury. A sprain can be a stretch, tear, or rip of muscle and can be any one of three grades, or degree of injury. With a mild sprain, Grade 1, the pain is local and tension in the muscle is increased. A moderate or Grade 2 sprain will show indications of reduced or impaired muscle function. With a severe or Grade 3 sprain, there is typically loss of muscle function. It is important to be aware of possible injuries a client may have recently sustained, and while gentle massage may be indicated for such injuries, always have a doctor examine the injury first.

70. B: The most common term in the medical field would be fibromyalgia. It is important for the massage therapist to know and understand medical terminology because it is the key to understanding the body and its pathology. This terminology is the means to speak a common language, which is familiar to all healthcare professionals. Miscommunications in terminology can lead to misunderstandings or more severe consequences to the patient. Understanding medical terminology will also help the therapist when writing treatment notes. When learning medical terminology, consider the parts of the word, for example, Fibro-, meaning fiber or fibrous and my-, meaning muscle. Knowing this we know that the term fibromyalgia is referring to the fibrous muscle tissue. The suffix, -algia means pain. Therefore, when a client states they have fibromyalgia, the therapist will know to be cautious not to cause more pain during the massage.

71. A: Cysts on the kidneys is a symptom rather than a part of the disease's etiology. The definition of etiology is then the incidence or situation in which a disease may occur. In this example, polycystic kidney disease is often hereditary with most cases exhibiting a mutation of the PKD1 gene. Additionally, research suggests that approximately 5% of patients with polycystic kidney disease are in end-stage renal disease. The etiology of a disease will vary depending on the disease, and may include anything from genetics to environmental causes. For example, emphysema, a respiratory disease, may have an etiology of environmental causes.

72. A: Tuberculosis is an airborne illness, meaning the disease is spread through the air, especially when an individual with the disease coughs or sneezes. For contagious diseases, there are a number of ways that the disease can be transmitted: through the air, blood, saliva, or sexual fluids. In order to prevent the healthcare workers from acquiring the disease, they must wear a mask. Blood-borne diseases may be spread through IV drug use, blood transfusions, or cuts. For a massage therapist, the best way to protect themselves from these types of illnesses is to be cautious and aware any cuts on their hands. If cuts or openings are present, then they should either wait until the cut is healed to massage or wear gloves.

73. B: Signs can be observed and measured. Coughing blood, fever, chills, and weight loss, all can be seen by outside observers and measures. On the other hand, chest pain would be referred to as a symptom, which is something that is subjective and only felt by the patient. Diseases contain both signs and symptoms and these words are often used interchangeably. As a massage therapist, you will never diagnose an individual, however if someone complains to you about various symptoms or you see signs that are questionable, you can also suggest they see their primary care physician.

74. A: Massage releases serotonin as well as dopamine. The release of serotonin regulates moods and allows the appropriate emotions to be displayed during any specific situation. Serotonin also effects in the individual in terms of calming. In an individual with depression, their serotonin is low. When serotonin is released, it may level out the depressed mood. Other psychological issues such as obsessive-compulsive disorders, chronic pain disorders, and eating disorders are also indicated by lower levels of serotonin, and may therefore benefit from massage. It is always important for a massage therapist to be aware of psychological problems and medication their clients are on, as some have adverse reactions to a calming massage.

75. C: The most appropriate massage technique for individuals with autism would be a firm, purposeful touch. These individuals, while some would think counter-intuitively, do like and want to be touched. However, for individuals with autism, their development disability is one in which social interactions are hindered and their days consist of a series of deliberate actions and behaviors. Therefore, massage should also be as such in order to make the client feel comfortable. Most importantly, a massage therapist must always respect the client and remain in constant communication during the massage, to ensure they are having a comfortable and beneficial experience.

76. A: Massage in general will influence the automatic nervous system and in a relaxation massage, this can be very calming, thus reducing the amount of anxiety felt by the client. Massage therapists must always remember to begin with a client based on where they are personally. For example, if a client comes into a massage with heightened anxiety, they may be resistant to gentle slow strokes at first. Therefore, the therapist should communicate with and respect the client in order to create a massage that is beneficial for them and helps ease their anxiety.

77. A: Individuals with osteoporosis have a serious bone disease. This disease results in a loss of bone density, specifically the loss of calcium, and is most typical in postmenopausal women. While its direct cause is unknown, osteoporosis has been linked to a decrease in the female hormone estrogen. Literally translated, osteoporosis means a porous bone. In some individuals, the condition will have progressed to a point where bone fractures can occur with no or little impact. Therefore, it is important for a therapist to be aware of any condition and adjust their massage accordingly.

78. B: The informed consent is the form required that gives the therapist permission to work on an individual. This form must be signed by a consenting adult or, in the case of body work for a minor, a legal guardian. It is important that the informed consent provides information about the nature of massage as well as information indicating that the individual has the right to refuse treatment at any point during the massage. By providing clients with this information, they have the opportunity to make an educated, informed decision on whether they want to receive treatment.

79. C: Transference occurs during a client-therapist relationship when the client transfers personal feelings onto the therapist. In this case the client may be seeing you as so much like their deceased spouse that they begin feeling for you what they felt of their spouse. As a massage therapist, this issue should be dealt with professionally and with sensitivity. If the client is unable to deal with these feelings in a healthy way, it would be most responsible for the therapist to refer the client to another massage therapist and/or grief counseling so they could learn to deal with the death of their spouse.

80. D: Countertransference occurs when a therapist places personal feelings on to their client. In this case as a therapist also recently dealing with the death of a loved one, you may find that your client reminds you of the deceased. It could also be that because of the similarities in your situations you may feel a superficial connection and attribute that connection to something deep. In this case, the best solution may be to be honest with your client and refer them to a different therapist.

81. B: Massaging your client's face would be crossing their personal boundaries. Personal boundaries will be different for everyone, and it is important to learn what these boundaries are for each client before beginning a massage. These are boundaries that we all set for ourselves on how close someone can get before we are no longer comfortable. In this situation, because your client stated prior to the massage that they did not like having their face massaged, then this clearly is a personal boundary. If a massage therapist ignores these things, then the massage will become an unpleasant experience for the client. Additionally, not all clients will say out loud what their boundaries are. By paying attention and watching for signs of discomfort, a therapist can ask questions and modify the massage to make sure the client is comfortable.

82. C: Listening and offering your own assessment of your client's situation is beyond a massage therapist's scope of practices and therefore would be considered crossing a legal and ethical boundary. It is important for a massage therapist to be empathic and show concern and sensitivity, especially for clients in vulnerable positions. However, a therapist can cause unwarranted damage if they offer services that they are unqualified to provide. In situations where a therapist crosses a legal boundary, they are at risk for not only harming their clients, but also harming their practice and may face legal actions.

83. A: Medical terminology is a set of terms, typically Latin or Greek that provides all healthcare professionals a common language. While not all massage therapists will work directly with a chiropractor or other medical professional, it will still be important for all to understand and know how to properly use medical terminology. There may be times throughout your career that you encounter a client with various health needs. In some cases, a physician, or other healthcare professional consultation will be necessary in order for you to provide the best and safest care to your client.

84. C: An independent contractor essentially is their own boss. While, as an independent contractor you may rent a room from a spa, you are still responsible for paying all of your own taxes; however, the rent you pay for the room rental could be deducted as a business expense. Independent contractors must keep careful records of all of their profits and losses, as all will be included on schedule C of their tax forms. In addition to keeping records, independent contractors are required to pay quarterly taxes, which is typically one quarter of the tax you expect to owe by the end of the year.

85. B: While not required in many European countries, draping is required by law for massage in the United States. This is a way the massage therapist can maintain their client's privacy and ensure the client is comfortable and warm throughout the massage. There are various techniques for draping; however, the main focus is to uncover only the body part you are working on. As noted, draping is also used to keep the client warm. Since as the client relaxes their body temperature may decrease, it is very easy to become cold during a massage. With this additional point in mind, therapists should also have extra blankets on hand.

86. A: Endangerment sites are locations on the body where the nerves are superficial. Pressure on these areas may cause the client extreme discomfort or potential damage to the underlying vessels and nerves. In addition to the armpit, the following are also considered endangerment sites: the eyes, inferior to the ear, the posterior cervical area, lymph nodes, the medial brachium, musculocutaneous nerve, median nerve, ulnar nerve, basilic vein, cubital areas of the median nerve, and radial and ulnar arteries and under the knees. Light strokes over these areas may be allowable; however, a massage therapist must always be careful and watch for signs of discomfort.

87. C: When discussing various conditions in terms of severity, healthcare workers will typically refer to the condition as acute or chronic. In this case, the back pain is chronic because it is existed for about a year. Had the client stated that his back problems began last week, the condition would be considered acute. Acute conditions will typically be short in duration; however, if a condition continues, it can become a chronic problem. As a massage therapist, it is important to understand if a client's conditions are acute or chronic so you know how to treat and track the problem.

88. C: If a client comes for a massage and is ill, the best thing of their therapist to do would be to refer them to a physician. Referrals are necessary in some cases because the therapist is not qualified to diagnosis or treat diseases. Referrals can also be used to enhance the client's treatment and healing. For example, you may refer a client to a chiropractor and suggest they have their back adjusted immediately following a massage. This would enhance the client's healing process. Because referrals are common in this field, it is important for therapists to be familiar with the various healthcare professionals in their area.

89. A: Confidentiality is the client's right to privacy. According to the Health Insurance Portability and Accountability Act of 1996, all healthcare professionals are required to maintain their client's confidentiality, which includes all massage therapists. When a new client comes in for a massage, it is the therapist's responsibility to inform the client about confidentiality and their rights to privacy. While therapists must maintain confidentiality, there may be situations were discussing a case is allowable; for example, when consulting with other healthcare professionals, if they are discussing clients with a supervisor for training or evaluation purposes, or if required by law.

90. B: S.O.A.P refers to Subjective Objective Assessment and Plan. With this form of note taking, the therapist will provide a range of information beginning with subjective information. This will consist completely of information that the client provides to the therapist. The subjective information will be what the therapist finds after working on the client. This could include information such as range of motion or observed signs of disorder. The assessment section of the documentation will include the outcomes of the session, for medical doctors, this section would include a diagnosis. Finally, the plan section of these notes will discuss the treatment plan.

91. C: Lymphatic massage would be contraindicated by a malignant neoplasm because this is a tumor or cancer that can be spread. Such tumors are abnormal growths, often caused by genetic conditions and are registered by the rest of the body as parasites. In many cases malignant neoplasms are spread through the lymphatic system and if massage if performed, the therapists may spread this disease to other parts of the body. The other type of tumor is a benign tumor, which is not spreadable. These tumors typically grow slower then malignant tumors and only become life-threatening if they grow to a size that hinders the functioning of surrounding organs.

92. A: Sprains are injuries to ligaments and are classified in three grades. In this case, the sprain would be classified as a Grade 1 sprain, which is mild and includes 0%-20% fiber tear. With this grade, the individual will continue to have normal range of motion by the area may be tender and slightly swollen. A Grade 2 sprain refers to a 20%-75% fiber tear, moderate resistance, swelling, muscle splinting, and a reduced range of motion. The final type of sprain is a Grade 3 sprain and refers to a 75%-100% fiber tear. This is a severe sprain that is painful and little to no motion.

93. C: Strains are injuries to muscles and tendons and are classified in three degrees. A first-degree strain results in 0%-10% fiber tear, mild pain and tenderness, and swelling. With a first-degree strain, the individual usually still has all normal functioning. A second-degree strain results in a 10%-50% fiber tear, pain, swelling, muscle splinting, and a reduced functioning. Finally, a third-degree strain results in a 50%-100% fiber tear, severe pain, swelling, and little to no muscle functioning. Regardless of the degree of the strain, massage is contraindicated for at least the first 24 hours after the injury and it may be beneficial for the therapist to refer the client for further evaluation and treatment prior to massaging the strained area.

94. B: A complete fracture is one in which the bone becomes completely separated. In addition to this type of fracture, other types of fractures include incomplete, closed, open, comminuted, compression, stress, greenstick, nonunion, malunion, delayed union, and spiral fractures. Of the more common fractures, the incomplete fracture results in a crack that does not go all the way through the bone. A closed fracture affects the bone but not the skin, while an open fracture affects both the bone and skin. A comminuted fracture results in the bone being cracked or splintered in more than one piece and a compression fracture is when the bone is pushed together, resulting in a fracture.

95. D: Cervicogenic headaches are related to various trigger points and would benefit from this type of massage. Symptoms of cervicogenic headaches may include altered neck posture and a limited range of motion. Other headache types include migraine, cluster, tension, and chronic daily. Migraine headaches are severe headaches with symptoms such as nausea and vomiting, extreme sensitivity to light, and eye pain. Cluster headaches are similar to migraine except these occur in clusters. Tension headaches are caused by muscle tension and may be relieved by massage; these headaches are not as severe as migraines. Chronic daily headaches can be caused from a number of things and specific treatment will depend on the cause of these headaches.

96. B: Hypovolemic shock is the result of a large amount of blood causing a decrease in blood pressure. While a hemorrhage is the most common cause of hypovolemic shock, the loss of interstitial fluid may also cause this type of shock. Cardiogenic shock may result from a variety of types of heart failure. Neurogenic shock results from the dilation of blood vessels, creating an unstable autonomic stimulation of smooth muscles. Anaphylactic shock is caused by an allergic reaction. A fifth type of shock includes a septic shock that is the result of septicemia, or the release of infectious toxins in the body.

97. D: Bronchitis is a lower respiratory tract infection because it occurs in the bronchi. With bronchitis, there is swelling of the bronchi due to infection and often the trachea is also infected. In these cases the disease is referred to as tracheobronchitis. This disease causes deep cough, typically with mucus and pus. Other lower respiratory tract infections include pneumonia, which is an infection in the lungs. Tuberculosis is a contagious disease that affects the lungs and surrounding tissues. Emphysema is caused from chronic bronchitis causing the alveoli to enlarge and rupture. Finally, asthma is the result of muscle spasms in the smooth muscles of the bronchial passages.

98. B: Hypernatremia is caused by sodium imbalance; specifically too much sodium. This is typically defined as above 145 mEq/L; hypernatremia could be cause by a high salt diet and may result in dehydration or diarrhea. On the other hand, hyponatremia would be too little sodium; typically below 136 mEq/L. Sodium imbalances affect the nervous system and include symptoms such as confusion, headaches, seizures, coma, and death. Potassium imbalances include levels less than 3.8 mEq/L and above 5.1 mEq/L. Small imbalances of potassium can result in serious illnesses. Calcium imbalances include any level less than 8.4 mg/dL or more than 10.5 mg/dL. Symptoms of calcium imbalances include muscle weakness, reduced reflexes, pancreatitis, and rickets.

99. A: Massage has been a part of healing techniques since approximately 3000 B.C. when the Chinese and Japanese wrote about Anma, or acupuncture. Acupuncture is the practice of placing needles on specific points of the body, specifically along the meridians to bring about pain relief. Acupuncture is used today along with variations of the technique including acupressure or shiatsu. Shiatsu, finger pressure, began in Japan in the 1900s. The focus of this therapeutic method is to balance the life energy that flows along the meridians. The therapist focuses on tsubo, or points along the channels, and finds stagnant points, which are an indication of disorder or pain.

100. B: The purpose of the massage therapist and the massage itself is to increase cell metabolism, decrease pain, and increase range of motion. It is not to heal. All healthcare professionals must work within the scope of their practice. For a massage therapist, diagnosing and treating disease is out of their scope of practice. However, many massage techniques will help with the healing process and it is beneficial if the therapist is in communication with the client's physician if they are being treated for other illnesses or conditions. This communication will provide the client with the best possible care.

101. A: Breaking up adhesions is considered a mechanical effect of massage. Mechanical effects are the result of applying direct pressure to the body. Other ways to create mechanical effects include assisted stretching techniques. Physiological effects are those that result in physical and chemical changes in the body. For example, a massage may help flush toxins and other waste products, which would increase blood flow and cellular metabolism. Psychological effects create an emotional change in the body. With massage, stimulation of the nervous system can reduce stress and increase relaxation and well being.

102. B: The lymphatic system relies on voluntary muscle movement in order to be moved throughout the body. This movement is important, as it is the lymph that is responsible for carrying waste and toxins from cell breakdown and metabolism out of the body. Massage is beneficial with this process, as it can assist with this movement. Just as massage increases blood circulation, it also increases lymphatic circulation. In addition, the flow of lymph out of the blood stream also increases because massage tends to open closed blood capillaries through the release of histamines and acetylcholine.

103. C: A muscle spasm or cramps can occur with overstimulation of the nervous system. In order to release a muscle spasm or cramp, it is suggested that the therapist perform compressions on the tendon of the muscle. This technique activates proprioceptors, which in turn release the spasm or cramp. Other techniques include slow stretching, stimulation of the Golgi tendons, and reciprocal inhibition treatments. Golgi tendons monitor the length of the muscles and react accordingly in order to bring a muscle back to normal. If the Golgi tendon senses that the muscle is overextended, it will contract; on the other hand, if the Golgi tendon senses that the muscle is too contracted, it will relax. In addition, Golgi tendons have inhibitory effects on muscles in order to maintain the normal position of the muscle.

104. C: Effleurage or gliding is typically the first stroke of a massage. This stroke helps to warm the muscles and help relax the client. With this massage stroke, the therapist's hands are firm but relaxed, and glide easily over the muscles. This stroke can also be used with the therapist's forearms, thumbs, or fists. Therapists should keep in mind that the effleurage stroke should be consistent in speed and pressure. Other uses for this massage stroke include to apply oil, assess your client's muscles, establish your client's pressure tolerance, stimulate muscles, stretch muscles, and to increase lymphatic flow.

105. A: Petrissage or kneading focuses on the deeper tissue and may involve lifting, rolling, and compressing the deep muscles. This stroke type is used sparingly as it can be exhausting for the therapist, however, proper body mechanics can assist in endurance. Petrissage strokes also include skin rolling, fulling, and ischemic compression. Petrissage is beneficial to the client in a number of ways including, increasing the removal of metabolic waste and other toxins, release adhesions in muscle bellies, increasing the flow of fluid in deep tissue, and stretching muscle tissue and fascia.

106. A: Range of motion is the natural movement that a joint can go through. Depending on the joint, its range of motion will vary. For example, The cervical joint has a range of motion from 0-80 degrees, shoulder from 0-180 degrees, elbow 0-140 degrees, radioulnar from 0-80 degrees, wrist from 0- 60, thoracic from 0-50 degrees, lumbar from 0-60 degrees, hip from 0-100 degrees, knee from 0-150 degrees, ankle from 0-40 degrees, subtalar from 0-30 degrees, and the metatarsophalangeal from 0-50 degrees. Note that the normal range of motion will also vary for each joint depending on the type of movement (e.g., flexion, extension, etc.). When a joint has abnormal restrictions its range of motion is reduced.

107. A: Massage is indicated for the treatment of asthma, as massage may be helpful in reducing stress and loosening intercostals, thus increasing breathing. Other conditions are contraindicated for massage and could result in further injury or problems. Edema, which is swelling, can be caused by a number of things; the massage therapist should ask questions in order to figure the cause, In the cases of edema due to heart decompensations, infection, kidney ailments, or obstructions, massage is contraindicated. Bursitis is inflammation of the bursae, and massage could increase the inflammatory response. Abdominal aneurysm is contraindicated on the abdomen. The therapist can massage other parts of the body not affected.

108. B: Hydrotherapy uses three forms of water: solid, liquid, and vapor, during the massage. In a hydrotherapy massage, water is introduced to the body, either externally or internally. The purpose or philosophy of hydrotherapy is to bring circulating blood to homeostasis, thus relieving the problem area. While water is the main tool in this form of massage therapy, a therapist may use heated poultices, masks, wraps, or baths to apply the water or to heat or cool the affected part of the body. The underlying theory behind hydrotherapy is that by changing the body temperature using water, healing can occur.

109. B: A systemic effect of hydrotherapy will affect the entire body. For example, vasodilation causes a drop in blood pressure throughout the entire body. A therapist may create a systemic effect by applying heat for 20-30 minutes. This heat application will continue to produce effects for up to an hour after the treatment. Local effects are restricted to specific areas of the body. Reflex affects the skin and other body parts through the nervous system. The various types of effects apply to both hot and cold applications. The results will depend on the type of treatment.

110. C: The study of movement is called Kinesiology. This field is often combined with biomechanics which looks at movement in terms of mechanics. Within this field, muscles are classified or termed according to their function. Prime movers are the muscles that initiate and maintain movement. Synergists assist the prime movers. Antagonists oppose the prime movers. The combination of a prime mover and an antagonist is referred to as a fixator. There are also neutralizers that inhibit unwarranted movement while the prime mover is in action. In addition to their functional classifications, there are different characteristics of muscles, including fast, slow, and intermediate twitch muscle fibers.

111. D: Specialized testing may include passive or active range of motion (ROM), strength testing, or orthopedic testing. The purpose of specialized tests is to determine the functionality of various areas of the body. Other parts of this type of assessment include taking a history including the client's family medical history, and personal medical history. Observations are also useful and should include mood, gait, and standing and sitting postures. A final component of this assessment includes palpation, which begins with the superficial tissue and gradually moves to the deeper tissues. With palpation, the therapist will feel for symmetry, temperature, muscle tone, and texture.

112. A: Wood is the element that is representative of the liver. The liver is considered a Yin organ. With TCM, each organ also has its own meridian. The liver meridian begins on the dorsal aspect of the big toe on the lateral side and travels up the body to the 6th intercostal space. It is important to note that all Yin meridians travel from the ground up. This organ may become dysfunctional when there is too much wind and dampness, and visible signs of disorder can be seen by yellowing of the eyes and the nails. Additionally, there are a number of disorders that may be treated on the liver meridian, including mood disorders, headaches, nausea, and vertigo.

113. C: Microvilli are found only in the small intestine and are organelles within the cytoplasmic membrane. The function of the microvilli is to increase the surface area of the small intestines and assist in absorption. These microvilli are a part of an extensive network of organelles that absorb fats from chime. Included in this process are lacteal, which are lymphatic vessels; plicae, circular folds; and villi, finger-like projections; all serving to increase the surface area of the small intestine and facilitate absorption. As materials enter into the small intestine, they travel through the duodenum, where most of the absorption occurs to the jejunum, and finally the ileum.

114. C: The permease system also called a cell or ion pump moves molecules against the concentration gradient. Because this movement is against the gradient, energy or ATP is required, thus it is an active transport system. Other active transport systems include pinocytosis, in which a cell will engulf liquid droplets and process them; and phagocytosis, or cell eating, in which a cell will engulf a solid molecule and process it. With phagocytosis, a cell will typically engulf bacteria or other cellular waste. Since ATP is required for these processes, the cells exert work and require chemical processes in order to create the energy required.

115. B: Amy will have to pay out-of-pocket expenses for the flood damage because she did not purchase Business & Personal Property Loss insurance. This type of insurance covers a business owner for a number of events including fires, water damage, or theft. Had Amy purchased this type of insurance, the insurance would have covered the loss of any business or personal equipment. While some events seem unlikely, it is important to understand the risks involved in owning a business as well as the precautions one can take to protect all business and personal assets.

116. B: Amy is covered in this case because she has Property Damage and Bodily Injury Liability. With this type of insurance, incidents that occur at her office including falls or slips as well as injury due to equipment failure are covered. This type of insurance is required in many states and may be specifically be required by a landlord if a therapist rents office space for their practice. In addition to covering a client in the case of an accident, this insurance protects the therapist from unwarranted bills or legal actions.

117. C: Amy did not develop a business plan. This is an essential document for any business, as it includes important information about the business, and its mission and goals. A typical business plan will include the following information: cover page, table of contents, owner's statement, executive summary, purpose and goals, a detailed description of the business, a marketing plan, risk assessment and financial analysis, operations and organizational policies, strategies for success, and other supporting information that the owner feels is necessary. While others may not read this document, it is important to have and keep updated in order to ensure you are on track with your business goals and you are able to refine these goals as the business grows.

118. B: By creating a logo and marketing materials, Amy is developing her professional image. Your professional image is the outward image presented to the public and your clients. It is important for therapists to represent themselves in a professional manner. Other ways a massage therapist can develop their professional image include keeping a clean massage room and waiting room, proper dress attire, and efficient and professional communication skills. A therapist's professional image will also expand to the therapeutic session itself, those who keep accurate notes, listen and are empathic toward their clients and respect their clients privacy show a positive professional image.

119. C: The occupational therapist would be the best referral in this case. The role of an occupational therapist is to work with clients to increase independence, thus increasing their quality of life. This type of therapist focuses on activities typically performed at work, in the home, or related to self care. It is an Occupational Therapist's job to enhance the development of their clients functioning. While you may continue to work with the client, the referral and continued communication with the other therapist would be essential in providing the client the best care possible.

120. A: Airway, Breathing, Circulation are the ABCs of First Aid. This is considered the primary survey and should be conducted immediately after finding a victim. If the individual is in any immediate danger, First Aid protocol states that you address any problem and then move on a secondary survey or assessment. The secondary survey will be more thorough and will include a full body survey to search for any injuries. It is important that both the primary and the secondary surveys are completed and are efficient as these precautions could be life-saving as the victim waits for emergency medical help.

121. B: An asymmetric standing position is the most efficient position for a massage therapist. For this position, the therapist will stand with one foot in front of the other. This will allow the therapist to leverage their own body weight into the massage. Additionally, as body weight is shifted from one foot to the other, the therapist can conserve energy. This position also protects the ankle and foot and allows for the knees to be bent throughout the massage. It is also beneficial to sit when possible while performing massage in order to conserve energy.

122. B: Passive joint movements also referred to as arthrokinematic movement occur as a result of another movement. This type of passive movement could also be considered the "play" a joint has or its ability to move freely within the joint capsule. Typically resulting after active movements, this accessory movement may slide, roll, or spin within a joint. On the other hand, active joint movements, or osteokinematic movements are voluntary and require effort to perform. For example flexing the arm is considered an osteokinematic movement. In massage, the therapist may perform various movements through stretching.

123. C: The anatomic barrier is the point at which injury would occur to a joint. Each joint's anatomic barrier will vary and is expressed as degrees for range of motion. However, because it is at this barrier that injury will occur, other barriers exist to avoid reaching the anatomic barrier. The physiologic barrier is determined by sensory functions of the nervous system. The physiologic barrier allows for full range of motion and full functionality of the joint. In addition to this barrier, there is the pathologic barrier that hinders normal range of motion. This may be expressed as stiffness or pain in the joint.

124. B: Bodywork serves to create wholeness within the individuals, including the mind, body, and the spirit. Through bodywork and with the use of various complementary systems of bodywork, an individual can find this interconnectedness. It is the responsibility of the therapist to respect the client and meet them where they are both physically and mentally. This will help put the client at ease and enable them to fully experience the benefits of massage and other complementary body work. Additionally, the therapist must understand his or her own limitations and feel comfortable to refer their clients to other practitioners when necessary.

125. B: All massage therapists should have a basic understanding of the functions and dysfunctions of the human body. However, for those therapists who are interested in working with physicians or within other medical settings, it will be even more important to understand these elements of the human body. It will be in these settings that the massage therapist will encounter a variety of illnesses and dysfunctions. As such, they must understand the indications, contraindications, and precautions that must be taken for each of their clients. These therapists may choose additional training in medical massage to ensure that they are knowledgeable to practice in this specialized field.

126. C: The effects of hydrotherapy are seen mostly within the autonomic nervous system. Depending upon the temperature of the water being used for the therapy, different aspects of this system will be stimulated. For example, to stimulate the sympathetic system, the therapist will use cold water, while they will use warm water to stimulate the parasympathetic responses. Additionally, by applying heat or cold for varying periods of time, the therapist can affect the dilatation of the circulatory system. More specifically, cold application for a short period of time will stimulate the nervous system and cause vasoconstriction.

127. C: Lymphatic drainage focuses on this system and helps move various toxins out of the body. While this is done naturally, manually manipulating the lymphatic system may cause a toxin overload and affect the client, causing them to feel fatigued. There are various modifications of lymphatic drainage including techniques developed my Emil Vodder, Eyal Lederman, and Bruno Chickly. However, regardless of the style used, this is a specialized massage technique that requires additional training. Lymph moves through the body through lymph vessels that are not controlled by the heart pump. Therefore the lymph vessels must contract in order to move the lymph through. Lymphatic drainage is one way to assist this system and drain toxins from the body.

128. B: Low blood pressure is contraindicated for lymphatic drainage because this type of body work lowers blood pressure. By performing for lymphatic drainage on a client who already has low blood pressure, dizziness and fainting may occur upon standing after the bodywork. Other contraindications include illnesses; both viral and bacterial infections. These are contraindicated because the lymphatic drainage may spread the illness to other parts of the body, thus enhancing the illness. In clients with fever, lymphatic drainage lowers body temperature. Finally, this type of body work affects the client's circulation and therefore those clients with weak hearts or other heart conditions may be contraindicated for lymphatic drainage.

129. C: Qi Gong is an oriental form of exercise that focuses on the breath. With these exercises, the individual practices the regulation of the breath, or Qi, through meditations and body positioning. These body positions are often performed as slow, deliberate movements and in some forms of Qi Gong, little or no movement is necessary. The purpose of this exercise is to increase the life force through the efficient circulation of the breath. This practice would be beneficial for both clients and massage therapists. Other oriental exercises including Dao Yin, Tai Ji Quan, and Tai Kwan Doe are also beneficial for maintaining balance between the mind, body, and spirit.

130. A: Palliative care focuses on making the client as comfortable as possible. In many cases those individuals in the end stages of a terminal illness will be uncomfortable and some may be in pain. As a massage therapist in this environment, you would be responsible for being empathic and respectful toward your client in order to ensure the body work was comforting and not causing additional pain. It will also be important that the therapist be in contact with the other healthcare professionals caring for the individual as well as the family.

131. B: The goal of shiatsu is balance. This form of bodywork affects both the nervous and lymphatic systems. Within the philosophy of shiatsu, the body consists of bioelectricity that moves from the top down and from the middle out. A therapist that practices this form of bodywork will focus on the energy behind the client's symptoms, rather than the symptoms themselves. Because shiatsu means finger pressure, there are a number of Shiatsu points on the body and in a typical session, the client will lie in a supine position while the therapist works their way through all points.

132. D: Systems are the most complex units of the body because they consist of all other units such as cells, tissues, and organs. Systems are comprised of organs that are arranged in such a way that they are able to work together to perform specific functions. Within the human body, there are eleven systems: integumentary; skeletal; muscular; nervous; endocrine; cardiovascular; lymphatic; respiratory; digestive; urinary; and reproductive. All systems are essential for maintaining balance and health. Because organs within a system function as a whole, when one organ is dysfunctional, the entire system will be affected.

133. C: Approximately 96% of the human body is comprised of oxygen, carbon, hydrogen, and nitrogen. These elements occur naturally and are essential for the proper functioning of our bodies. In addition to these main elements, there are nearly 20 other elements that can be found in very small quantities within the body. Elements are composed of atoms combining to form molecules. In addition to these elements, they can combine, typically through a chemical reaction, to form compounds. For example, carbon dioxide is formed in the lungs. This compound is formed by the fusion of two oxygen molecules.

134. C: Red blood cells do not have a nucleus as well as no cytoplasmic organelles. Also referred to as erythrocytes, these cells are responsible for transporting oxygen and carbon dioxide. Because these cells do not have a nucleus, they are unable to reproduce and only have a life span of approximately 80-120 days. The red pigment of these cells is caused by hemoglobin which is responsible for homoeostasis. Disorders of red blood cells often occur because the body overproduces these cells, resulting in disorders such as polycythemia. Other red blood cell disorders include anemia, which comes in a variety of forms.

135. A: Squamous epithelial tissue is flat and scale-like. This type of tissue can be found in the air sacs of the lungs. This tissue is typically seen as a very thin layer and is able to absorb oxygen and pass it into the blood stream. Other tissue types include the cuboidal, which is cube shaped, columnar, which is high and wide, and transitional, which is able to stretch and therefore may vary in shape. In addition to the types of epithelial tissues, they can also be found in varying arrangements including simple and stratified.

136. A: The integumentary system includes the body's oil glands as well as the skin, hair, nails, sense receptors, and sweat glands. This system accounts for approximately 16% of the average person's body weight and may weigh approximately 20 pounds for an average-size adult. This system is the body's first line of defense against toxins and other contaminants as well as protects the organs from physical damage. The oil glands in this system serve to provide moisture to the skin. Also included in this system are sense organs and other sensors that serve to regulate the body and maintain homeostasis.

137. B: There are a number of risk factors for disease, some of which can be controlled for and some which cannot be controlled for. Those that cannot be controlled for include genetic factors. These risk factors are passed on from generation to generation in the DNA. On the other hand, risk factors such as lifestyle, stress, and environment can be controlled for. For example, lifestyle risk factors such as smoking, excessive sun tanning, and poor diet will put an individual at a higher risk of some diseases. Stress can also increase one's risk for disease. Finally, although not all environmental conditions can be controlled for, it is possible for humans to change their environment in order to reduce risk factors.

138. B: Serous membranes are found within closes cavities. This type of membrane is made up of two thin layers of tissue, one layer being simple squamous and the other layer being connective tissue. The connective tissue, which is on the bottom, serves to support cells. These membranes are named specifically based on their location in the body. For example, the serous membranes that cover body cavities are called parietal, whereas those that cover organs are called visceral. These membranes serve to reduce friction between organs by producing and releasing a lubricant.

139. C: The mucous membranes are those that open to the outside of the body. This will include the respiratory, digestive, urinary, and reproductive tracts. The makeup of mucous membranes will depend on the location of the membrane and can range from stratified squamous membranes found in the esophagus, to simple columnar membranes found in the digestive tract. These membranes remain moist due to the thick mucus of which they are comprised. In addition, the point at which the skin and the mucus membrane meet is referred to as mucocutaneous and are typically located around openings on the body.

140. C: Myofilaments are structures or units within each skeletal muscle fiber. Within each muscle fiber, myofilaments may be thick or thin. Thick myofilaments produce the protein myosin, whereas thin myofilaments produce the protein actin. Additionally, the unit of both thick and thin myofilaments is referred to as a sarcomere. As the muscle contracts the myofilaments attach and pull on each other. As the muscle relaxes, the myofilaments release. Calcium and energy, supplied by the breakdown of ATP, are both necessary for this process to work. This is also known was the sliding filament model.

141. D: There are four main muscles of the trunk and from deep to superior are transversus abdominis, internal oblique, rectus abdominis, and external oblique. The transversus abdominis, internal oblique, and external oblique muscles function to compress the abdomen and all have an insertion point at the midline of the abdomen. The external oblique muscles have an origin at the lower thoracic cage. The internal oblique muscles have an origin at the pelvis. The transversus abdominis has an origin at the ribs, vertebrae, and the pelvis. Finally, the rectus abdominis functions to flex the trunk and has an insertion at the lower rib cage and an origin at the pubis.

142. C: The Iliopsoas is not a part of the adductor group for the lower extremities. Rather, this muscle serves to flex the thigh or the trunk and has an insertion at the femur and an origin at the ilium and vertebrae. Additionally, this muscle functions to stabilize the trunk. The adductor longus, gracilis, and pectineus are all adductor muscles. The adductor longus and the pectineus have an insertion at the femur and an origin at the pubis. The gracilis has an insertion at the tibia and an origin at the pubis.

143. B: The biceps femoris is a part of the hamstring group that functions to flex the knee. This muscle has an insertion at the tibia and an origin at the ischium. Other muscles in this group include the semimembranosus with an insertion at the tibia and an origin at the ischium and the semitendinosus, with an insertion at the fibula and an origin at the ischium and femur. For a runner, these muscles are very important because they work while running. Injury to muscles in the hamstring groups often occur due to strain, or overexertion of the muscle, or pulling one of the muscles.

144. C: The epiphyseal plate is not found in the long bone of an adult. Rather, what is found is the epiphyseal line. The difference between the two is that the epiphyseal plate is made of cartridge and the epiphyseal line has become ossified bone. This ossification of bone occurs during growth and once all of the cartilage has turned into bone, growth stops. Other structures in the long bone include the epiphysis (at the end), spongy bone (found in the epiphysis), red marrow (in the spongy bone), compact bone (consisting of the diaphysis), the periosteum and endosteum (outer and inner layers), and the medullary cavity (hollow inner part of the long bone).

145. B: A tuberosity is a bony landmark characterized by its large round projection. Massage therapists may use these bony landmarks to find muscles as the massage. Other bony landmarks include tubercles, which are small and knob-like, and the trochanter, which is found on the femur. Other landmarks such as a crest (ridge or bone, found on the ilium), line (less prominent than a crest, on the femur), epicondyle (raised area), spine (sharp projections), malleolus (projections which are both medial and lateral such as the ankle bones), and a process (prominent projections on a bone) can also be used to locate muscles and their attachments.

146. C: A neutralizer refers to the counteraction of one muscle in order to avoid undesired movements. On the other hand, there are five main functions of bones: first, to support the body, including the organs and the muscles; to protect the organs from injury, specifically the skull completely covers the brain and the rib cage covers the lungs and heart; to function for movement; to serve as storage for calcium; and finally, to conduct the process of hemopoiesis, the process of developing blood cells.

147. B: Pronation is the movement that will result in the palms facing toward the back when beginning in the anatomical position. In this case, by turning the arms again so the palms face forward is supination. These positions are also referred to during a massage. For example, when a client is lying face-down, they are in the prone position. When the client is laying face up on their backs, they are in the supine position. While a therapist may not use these terms when communicating with their clients, these may be referred to in the assessment and session notes as well as in consultation with other healthcare professionals.

148. B: Muscle fibers respond as all-or-none. In other words, if the muscle fiber contracts, then the entire fiber contracts fully before it can relax. A threshold stimulus refers to the minimum stimulus that can be applied to a muscle fiber before it reacts. Once the threshold stimulus is to a level where the muscle will react, it will be an all-or-none response. When discussing muscle movement, the prime mover refers to the main muscle contracting in order to move the body. At the same time the antagonist relaxes while the prime mover is contracting, facilitating the movement.

149. D: The spinal cord is a part of the nervous systems, however, not the brain. The cerebrum is located in the upper-most portion of the brain and is the largest section. This section is divided into the left and right lobes or hemispheres. The cerebellum is located posterior to the cerebrum, also has two hemispheres, and is made up of gray matter on the outside and white matter on the inside. The diencephalon is positioned between the cerebrum and the midbrain and surrounds the third ventricle. Included in the diencephalon are the thalamus and the hypothalamus.

150. C: There are twelve pairs of cranial nerves in the human body. Eleven of these nerves originate under the brain's surface and travel down through the brain stem and spinal cord. However, the one exception is one pair of cranial nerves that begins in the cerebrum. As the cranial nerves travel through the spinal cord, they branch off from one of thirty-one segments in the spinal cord to various parts of the head, neck, and body. Moving from top to bottom, sections of the spinal cord branch off, allowing the nerves to reach the body, including the conus medullaris, filum terminale, and the cauda equine.

151. B: Deep sensory receptors are located in the muscles, tendons, and joints. The superficial receptors are located on the skin and the mucosa, and sense events such as temperature, pressures, and pain at the surface of the body. Visceral receptors, located in the viscera, sense things like hunger and visceral pain. Pain receptors will sense visceral, somatic, and referred pain. A fifth type of sensory receptor is the special receptor located in the eyes, ears, mouth, and nose, which function as our senses.

152. A: Antidiuretic hormone targets the kidney tissues. The purpose of this hormone is to reduce the excretion of water. What is occurring when this hormone is released is the kidneys are putting urine back into the blood stream. This action may be necessary if the body must conserve water, for example, in cases of dehydration. Essentially, the antidiuretic hormone comes from the posterior pituitary gland and works on the diuretic, which produces water and urine, and thus stops production. This hormone is also referred to as the "water-retaining hormone" or the "urine-decreasing hormone."

153. B: Epinephrine is produced in the adrenal medulla. This hormone targets the sympathetic nervous system. The result of this hormone being released is an increase in heart rate, blood pressure, and blood glucose levels. Additionally, breathing rate will increase as the airways dilate. Finally, individuals experience a reduction of digestion. Another hormone produced by the adrenal medulla is norepinephrine. This hormone has the same functions and actions as epinephrine. These hormones may be necessary if an individual has not eaten and their blood glucose levels drop, with the release of epinephrine, the blood glucose level will increase for a short period of time until the individual has a chance to eat.

154. C: Plasma is the liquid portion of blood. Plasma is necessary for the transport of oxygen from the respiratory organs and other vital minerals and nutrients from the digestive organs. Plasma also serves to carry waste products out of the body. Plasma makes up a large portion of the blood, approximately 55%. Within the plasma, approximately 7% is protein, 91% of the plasma is water, and the remaining 2% consists of other solutes. The remainder of the blood is made up of various cell formations called formed elements. These formed elements include platelets, leukocytes, and erythrocytes.

155. A: Providing your clients with an intake form is the best way for you to gather all necessary information. Intake forms commonly include the client's name and contact information and a brief medical questionnaire containing the most common conditions. Additionally, this form may also include the confidentiality notice which is to be signed by the client. In addition to the intake form, a therapist may choose to also ask questions if clarification on any item is necessary. It is important to take the time before a massage to learn about each client. With repeat clients, while an intake form may not be necessary every time, it will be necessary of the therapist to ask questions about any changes in their health or existing conditions.

156. A: Ayurveda is the massage technique that includes the Vata, Pitta, and Kapha. Ayurveda is a traditional Indian form of massage that translates to "the science of life." The Vata, Pitta, and Kapha are three doshas of Ayurveda that refer to motion, energy production, and structure, respectively. Each dosha describes a body type. The Vata is a slender body type with prominent features. These individuals typically are cold and have dry skin. Pitta is a medium body type full of strength. Finally, the Kapha is a heavy body type. These individuals are solid, may be overweight and have a tendency toward slow digestion. The treatment of an individual undergoing Ayurveda will depend on their dosha.

157. C: The massage technique Lomi-Lomi is characteristic of its broad, long movements. This technique originates from the South Pacific and incorporates prayer and the notion of a higher power. Therapists practicing Lomi-Lomi will also use palms, their feet, sticks, and stones throughout the massage. It is suggested that this technique aids in digestion, can be restorative, and is often used by native healers. This form of massage rests on the philosophy that all living things seek love and harmony. By creating balance and harmony within the body, you can also create these aspects in your everyday life.

158. A: A stone massage will result in the conduction of heat. Conduction occurs when there is direct contact and heat is transferred. Using a sauna would be an example of convection, by which heat is transferred by increasing the surrounding air temperature. As the sauna temperature increases, your body temperature will also increase. Using an ultrasound is an example of conversion. In the case of the ultrasound, energy is being converted into a different type of energy in order to create heat. These three types of heat transfer: conduction, convection, and conversion, are all examples of thermal effects of heat.

159. B: A sitz bath is a bath in which only the pelvic region is exposed to the water. There are three main types of sitz baths including a hot sitz, cold sitz, and a contrast sitz. In the hot sitz bath the client would be exposed to water temperature of 105-115 degrees Fahrenheit. Therapists must remember that the client must be comfortable with the water temperature. In a clod sitz bath, the client will be exposed to water temperatures of 55-75 degrees Fahrenheit. A contrast sitz bath will include a hot phase and a cold phase. The alteration of the hot and cold would be three minutes of hot water and 30 seconds of cold water.

160. C: Active listening is a very important communication skill. This type of listening will allow you to remember more of what the client says and will let the client know that you are listening and you care about their situation. Demonstrating caring and understanding will be an important step to developing trust in the therapist-client relationship. When this trust is developed the client will ultimately feel more comfortable with the therapist and will be able to relax more during the massage and receive more benefit from the work. While being aware of your clients' various conditions is important, tools such as the client intake form will help provide you, the therapist, with that information.

Special Report: Musculature/Innervation Review of the Arm and Back

Muscle	Origin	Insertion	Nerve
Trapezius	Ext. Occipit Protuberance, Spines of T Vertebrae	Lateral Clavicle, Spine of the Scapula	Spinal Accessory Nerve CN XI
Latissimus Dorsi	Spines of Lower 6 T Vertebrae, Iliac Crest and Lower 4 Ribs	Bicipital Groove	Thoracodorsal
Levator Scapulae	Transverse Process of C1-C4	Upper Medial Border of Scapula	Dorsal Scapula
Rhomboid Major	Spinous Process of T2-T5	Medial Border Scapula Below Spine	Dorsal Scapular
Rhomboid Minor	Spinous Process of C7-T1	Medial Border Scapula Opp. Spine	Dorsal Scapular
Teres Major	Lateral Dorsal Inferior Angle of Scapula	Bicipital Groove	Lower Subscapular
Teres Minor	Lateral Scapula 2/3 way down	Greater Tubercle of Humerus	Axillary
Deltoid	Lateral 1/3 Clavicle and Acromion Process, Spine of the Scapula	Deltoid Tuberosity	Axillary
Supraspinatus	Supraspinatus Fossa	Greater Tubercle of Humerus	Suprascapular
Infraspinatus	Infaspinatus Fossa	Greater Tubercle of Humerus	Suprascapular
Subscapularis	Subscapular Fossa	Lesser Tubercle of Humerus	Upper and lower Subscapular
Serratus Anterior	Slips of Upper 8-9 Ribs	Ventral-Medial Border Scapula	Long Thoracic
Subclavius	Inferior Surface of the Clavicle	First Rib	Nerve to the Subclavius
Pectoralis Major	Medial ½ clavicle and Side of Sternum	Bicipital Groove	Medial and Lateral Pectoral
Pectoralis Minor	Ribs 3,4,5 or 2,3,4	Coracoid Process	Medial Pectoral
Biceps Branchii	Supraglenoid Tubercle	Posterior Margin of Radial Tuberosity	Musculocutaneous
Coracobrachialis	Coracoid Process	Medial Humerus at Deltoid Tuberosity Level	Musculocutaneous
Brachialis	Anterior-Lateral ½ of Humerus	Ulnar Tuberosity and Coronoid Process	Musculocutaneous

Triceps Brachii	Infraglenoid Tubercle, Below and Medial to the Radial Groove	Olecranon Process	Radial
Anconeus	Posterior, Lateral Humeral Condyle	Upper Posterior Ulna	Radial
Brachioradialis	Lateral Supracondylar Ridge of Humerus	Radial Styloid Process	Radial
Pronator Teres	Medial Epicondyle and Supracondylar Ridge	½ Way Down on Lateral Radius	Median
Pronator Quadratus	Distal-Medial Ulna	Distal-Lateral Radius	Anterior Interosseous

Musculature/Innervation Review of the Forearm

Muscle	Origin	Insertion	Nerve
Brachioradialis	Lateral Supracondylar Ridge of Humerus	Radial Styloid Process	Radial
Pronator Teres	Medial Epicondyle and Supracondylar Ridge	½ Way Down on Lateral Radius	Median
Pronator Quadratus	Distal-Medial Ulna	Distal-Lateral Radius	Anterior Interosseous
Supinator	Lateral Epicondyle of Humerus	Upper ½ Lateral, Posterior Radius	Posterior Inter-Deep Radial
Flexor Carpi Radialis	Medial Epicondyle of Humerus	2nd and 3rd Metacarpal	Median
Flexor Carpi Ulnaris	Medial Epicondyle of Humerus	Pisiform, Hamate, 5th Metacarpal	Ulnar
Palmaris Longus	Medial Epicondyle of the Humerus	Palmar Aponeurosis and Flexor Retinaculum	Median
Flexor Digitorum Suerficialis	Medial Epicondyle, Radius, Ulna	Medial 4 Digits	Median
Flexor Digitorum Profundus	Ulna, Interosseous Membrane	Medial 4 Digits (distal part)	Median (lateral 2 digits), Ulnar (median 2 digits)
Flexor Pollicis Longus	Radius	Distal Phalanx (thumb)	Anterior Inter-Deep Median
Extensor Carpi Radialis Longus	Lateral Condyle and Supracondylar Ridge	2nd Metacarpal	Radial
Extensor Carpi Radialis Brevis	Lateral Epicondyle of Humerus	3rd Metacarpal	Posterior Inter-Deep Radial
Extensor Carpi Ulnaris	Lateral Epicondyle of Humerus	5th Metacarpal	Posterior Inter-Deep Radial

Extensor Digitorum	Lateral Epicondyle of Humerus	Extension Expansion Hood of Medial 4 Digits	Posterior Inter-Deep Radial
Extensor Digiti Minimi	Lateral Epicondyle of Humerus	Extension Expansion Hood of (little finger)	Posterior Inter-Deep Radial
Abductor Pollicis Longus	Posterior Radius and Ulna	Radial Side of 1st Metacarpal	Posterior Inter-Deep Radial
Extensor Indicis	Ulna and Interosseous Membrane	Extension Expansion Hood (index finger)	Posterior Inter-Deep Radial
Extensor Pollicis Longus	Ulna and Interosseous Membrane	Distal Phalanx (thumb)	Posterior Inter-Deep Radial
Extensor Pollicis Brevis	Radius	Proximal Phalanx (thumb)	Posterior Inter-Deep Radial

Musculature/Innervation Review of the Hand

Muscle	Origin	Insertion	Nerve
Adductor Policis	Capitate and Base of Adjacent Metacarpals	Proximal Phalanx (thumb)	Deep Branch of Ulnar
Lumbricals	Tendons of Flexor Digitorum Profundas	Extension Expansion Hood of Medial 4 Digits	Deep Branch Ulnar (medial 2 Ls), Median (lateral 2 Ls)
Dorsal Interosseous Muscles (4)	Sides of Metacarpals	Extension Expansion Hood of Digits 2-4	Deep Branch Ulnar
Palmar Interosseous (3)	Sides of Metacarpals	Extension Expansion Hood, Digits 2,4,5	Deep Branch Ulnar
Palmaris Brevis	Anterior Flexor Retinaculum and Palmar Aponeurosis	Skin-Ulnar Border of Hand	Superficial Ulnar
Abductor Pollicis Brevis	Flexor Retinaculum, Trapezium	Lateral Proximal Phalanx (thumb)	Median (thenar branch)
Flexor Pollicis Brevis	Flexor Retinaculum, Trapezium	Lateral Proximal Phalanx (thumb)	Median (thenar branch)
Opponens Pollicis	Flexor Retinaculum, Trapezium	Radial Border (1st Metacarpal)	Median (thenar branch)
Abductor Digiti Minimi	Flexor Retinaculum, Pisiform	Proximal Phalanx (little finger)	Deep Branch Ulnar
Flexor Digiti Minimi	Flexor Retinaculum, Hamate	Proximal Phalanx (little finger)	Deep Branch Ulnar
Opponens Digiti Minimi	Flexor Retinaculum, Hamate	Ulnar Medial Border (5th Metacarpal)	Deep Branch Ulnar

Musculature/Innervation Review of the Thigh

Muscle	Origin	Insertion	Nerve
Psoas Major	Bodies and Discs of T12-L5	Lesser Trochanter	L2,3
Psoas Minor	Bodies and Discs of T12 and L1	Pectineal Line of Superior Pubic Bone	L2,3
Iliacus	Upper 2/3 Iliac Fossa	Lesser Trochanter	Femoral L2-4
Pectinius	Pubic Ramus	Spiral Line	Femoral
Iliposoas	Joining of Psoas Major and Iliacus	Lesser Trochanter	L2-4
Piriformis	Anterior Surface of the Sacrum	Greater Trochanter	S1, S2
Obturator Internus	Inner Surface of the Obturator Membrane	Greater Trochanter	Sacral Plexus
Obturator Externus	Outer Surface of the Obturator Membrane	Greater Trochanter	Obturator
Gemellus Superior	Ischial Spine	Greater Trochanter	Sacral Plexus
Gemellus Inferior	Ischial Tuberosity	Greater Trochanter	Sacral Plexus
Quadratus Femoris	Ischial Tuberosity	Quadrate Tubercle of the Femur	Sacral Plexus
Gluteus Maximus	Outer Surface of Ilium, Sacrum and Coccyx	Iliotibial Tract, Gluteal Tubercle of the Femur	Inferior Gluteal
Gluteus Minimus	Outer Surface of the Ilium	Greater Trochanter	Superior Gluteal
Gluteus Medius	Outer Surface of the Ilium	Greater Trochanter	Superior Gluteal
Satorius	Anterior Superior Iliac Spine	Upper Medial Tibia	Femoral
Quadriceps Femoris	Anterior Inferior Iliac Spine, Femur-Lateral and Medial	Tibial Tuberosity	Femoral
Gracilis	Pubic Bone	Upper Medial Tibia	Obturator (anterior branch)
Adductor Longus	Pubic Bone	Linea Aspera	Obturator (anterior branch)
Adductor Brevis	Pubic Bone	Linea Aspera	Obturator (anterior branch)
Abductor Magnus	Pubic Bone	Entire Linea Aspera	Sciatic, Obturator
Tensor Faciae Latae	Iliac Crest	Iliotibial Band	Superior Gluteal
Biceps Femoris	Ischial Tuberosity, Linea Aspera	Head of Fibula, Lateral Condyle of Tibia	Sciatic-Tibial portion and Common Peroneal Portion
Semimembranosus	Ischial Tuberosity	Upper Medial Tibia	Sciatic-Tibial Portion
Semitendinosus	Ischial Tuberosity	Upper Medial Tibia	Sciatic-Tibial Portion

Musculature/Innervation Review of the Calf and Foot

Muscle	Origin	Insertion	Nerve
Tibialis Anterior	Upper 2/3 Lateral Tibia and Interosseous Membrane	1st Cuneiform and Base of 1st Metatarsal	Deep Peroneal
Extensor Digitorum Longus	Upper 2/3 Fibula and Interosseous Membrane	4 Tendons-Distal Middle Phalanges	Deep Peroneal
Extensor Hallucis Longus	Middle 1/3 of Anterior Fibula	Base of Distal Phalanx of Big Toe	Deep Peroneal
Peroneus Tertius	Distal Fibula	Base of 5th Metatarsal	Deep Peroneal
Extensor Hallucis Brevis	Dorsal Calcaneus	Extensor Digitorum Longus Tendons	Deep Peroneal
Peroneus Longus	Upper 2/3 Lateral Fibula	1st Metatarsal and 1st Cuneiform	Superficial Peroneal
Peroneus Brevis	Lateral Distal Fibula	5th Metatarsal Tuberosity	Superficial Peroneal
Soleus	Upper Shaft of Fibula	Calcaneus via Achilles Tendon	Tibial
Flexor Digitorum Longus	Middle 1/3 of Posterior Tibia	Base of Distal Phalanx of Lateral 4 Toes	Tibial
Flexor Hallucis Longus	Middle and Lower 1/3 of Posterior Tibia	Distal Phalanx of Big Toe	Tibial
Tibialis Posterior	Posterior Upper Tibia, Fibula	Navicular Bone and 1st Cuneiform	Tibial
Popliteus	Upper Posterior Tibia	Lateral Condyle of Femur	Tibial
Flexor Digitorum Brevis	Calcaneus	Middle Phalanges of Lateral 4 Toes	Medial Plantar
Abductor Hallucis	Calcaneus	Medial Proximal Phalanx of Big Toe	Medial Plantar
Abductor Digiti Brevis	Calcaneus	Lateral Proximal Phalanx of Big Toe	Lateral Plantar
Quadratus Plantae	Lateral and Medial Side of the Calcaneus	Tendons of Flexor Digitorum Longus	Lateral Plantar
Lumbricals	Tendons of Flexor Digitorum Longus	Extensor Tendons of Toes	Medial Plantar/Lateral Plantar
Flexor Hallucis Brevis	Cuboid Bone	Splits on Base of Proximal Phalanx of Big Toe	Medial Plantar
Flexor Digiti Minimi Brevis	Base of 5th Metatarsal	Base of Proximal Phalanx of Little Toe	Lateral Plantar

Abductor Hallucis	Metatarsals 2-4	Base of Proximal Phalanx of Big Toe	Lateral Plantar
Interossei	Sides of Metatarsal Bones	Base of 1st Phalanx and Extensor Tendons	Lateral Plantar

CPR Guidelines for Professional Rescuers

Topic	Adult	Child	Infant
	Past puberty	1 y/o - puberty	Under 1 y/o
Conscious Choking	abdominal thrusts (or chest thrusts in pregnant/obese)	abdominal thrusts	5 back slaps and 5 chest thrusts in infant
Unconscious Choking	Begin chest compression. Look in the victim's mouth for foreign body before giving breaths.		
Rescue Breaths Normal breath given over 1 second until chest rises.	10-12 breaths per minute (1 breath every 6-8 seconds)	12-20 breaths per minute (1 breath every 3-5 seconds)	20 breaths per minute (1 breath every 3 seconds)
Chest Compressions to Ventilation Ratios (Single Rescuer)	30:2		
Chest Compressions to Ventilation Ratios (Two Rescuer)	30:2	15:2	
Chest Compression rate	At least 100/minute		
Chest Compression Land Marking Method	two hands center of the chest, even with nipples	one hand center of the chest even with nipples	2 or 3 fingers, just below the nipple line at the center of the chest
Chest Compression Depth	At least 2" compression (hands overlapping)	about 2" compression or 1/3 the AP diameter (only heel of one hand)	about 1 ½" compression or 1/3 the AP diameter (2 fingers)
Activate Emergency Response System	As soon as you realize that the victim is unresponsive	After 5 cycles of CPR	After 5 cycles of CPR

Checklist:

- Check the scene
- Check for responsiveness – ask, "Are you OK?"
- Adult - call 911, then administer CPR
- Child/Infant – administer CPR for 5 cycles, then call 911
- Open victim's airway and check for breathing
- Two rescue breaths should be given, 1 second each, and should produce a visible chest rise
- If the air does not go in, reposition and try 2 breaths again
- Check victim's pulse – chest compressions are recommended if an infant or child has a rate less than 60 per minute with signs of poor perfusion
- Continue 30:2 ratio until victim moves, AED is brought to the scene, or professional help arrive

How to Overcome Test Anxiety

Just the thought of taking a test is enough to make most people a little nervous. A test is an important event that can have a long-term impact on your future, so it's important to take it seriously and it's natural to feel anxious about performing well. But just because anxiety is normal, that doesn't mean that it's helpful in test taking, or that you should simply accept it as part of your life. Anxiety can have a variety of effects. These effects can be mild, like making you feel slightly nervous, or severe, like blocking your ability to focus or remember even a simple detail.

If you experience test anxiety—whether severe or mild—it's important to know how to beat it. To discover this, first you need to understand what causes test anxiety.

Causes of Test Anxiety

While we often think of anxiety as an uncontrollable emotional state, it can actually be caused by simple, practical things. One of the most common causes of test anxiety is that a person does not feel adequately prepared for their test. This feeling can be the result of many different issues such as poor study habits or lack of organization, but the most common culprit is time management. Starting to study too late, failing to organize your study time to cover all of the material, or being distracted while you study will mean that you're not well prepared for the test. This may lead to cramming the night before, which will cause you to be physically and mentally exhausted for the test. Poor time management also contributes to feelings of stress, fear, and hopelessness as you realize you are not well prepared but don't know what to do about it.

Other times, test anxiety is not related to your preparation for the test but comes from unresolved fear. This may be a past failure on a test, or poor performance on tests in general. It may come from comparing yourself to others who seem to be performing better or from the stress of living up to expectations. Anxiety may be driven by fears of the future—how failure on this test would affect your educational and career goals. These fears are often completely irrational, but they can still negatively impact your test performance.

Elements of Test Anxiety

As mentioned earlier, test anxiety is considered to be an emotional state, but it has physical and mental components as well. Sometimes you may not even realize that you are suffering from test anxiety until you notice the physical symptoms. These can include trembling hands, rapid heartbeat, sweating, nausea, and tense muscles. Extreme anxiety may lead to fainting or vomiting. Obviously, any of these symptoms can have a negative impact on testing. It is important to recognize them as soon as they begin to occur so that you can address the problem before it damages your performance.

The mental components of test anxiety include trouble focusing and inability to remember learned information. During a test, your mind is on high alert, which can help you recall information and stay focused for an extended period of time. However, anxiety interferes with your mind's natural processes, causing you to blank out, even on the questions you know well. The strain of testing during anxiety makes it difficult to stay focused, especially on a test that may take several hours. Extreme anxiety can take a huge mental toll, making it difficult not only to recall test information but even to understand the test questions or pull your thoughts together.

Effects of Test Anxiety

Test anxiety is like a disease—if left untreated, it will get progressively worse. Anxiety leads to poor performance, and this reinforces the feelings of fear and failure, which in turn lead to poor performances on subsequent tests. It can grow from a mild nervousness to a crippling condition. If allowed to progress, test anxiety can have a big impact on your schooling, and consequently on your future.

Test anxiety can spread to other parts of your life. Anxiety on tests can become anxiety in any stressful situation, and blanking on a test can turn into panicking in a job situation. But fortunately, you don't have to let anxiety rule your testing and determine your grades. There are a number of relatively simple steps you can take to move past anxiety and function normally on a test and in the rest of life.

Physical Steps for Beating Test Anxiety

While test anxiety is a serious problem, the good news is that it can be overcome. It doesn't have to control your ability to think and remember information. While it may take time, you can begin taking steps today to beat anxiety.

Just as your first hint that you may be struggling with anxiety comes from the physical symptoms, the first step to treating it is also physical. Rest is crucial for having a clear, strong mind. If you are tired, it is much easier to give in to anxiety. But if you establish good sleep habits, your body and mind will be ready to perform optimally, without the strain of exhaustion. Additionally, sleeping well helps you to retain information better, so you're more likely to recall the answers when you see the test questions.

Getting good sleep means more than going to bed on time. It's important to allow your brain time to relax. Take study breaks from time to time so it doesn't get overworked, and don't study right before bed. Take time to rest your mind before trying to rest your body, or you may find it difficult to fall asleep.

Along with sleep, other aspects of physical health are important in preparing for a test. Good nutrition is vital for good brain function. Sugary foods and drinks may give a burst of energy but this burst is followed by a crash, both physically and emotionally. Instead, fuel your body with protein and vitamin-rich foods.

Also, drink plenty of water. Dehydration can lead to headaches and exhaustion, especially if your brain is already under stress from the rigors of the test. Particularly if your test is a long one, drink water during the breaks. And if possible, take an energy-boosting snack to eat between sections.

Along with sleep and diet, a third important part of physical health is exercise. Maintaining a steady workout schedule is helpful, but even taking 5-minute study breaks to walk can help get your blood pumping faster and clear your head. Exercise also releases endorphins, which contribute to a positive feeling and can help combat test anxiety.

When you nurture your physical health, you are also contributing to your mental health. If your body is healthy, your mind is much more likely to be healthy as well. So take time to rest, nourish your body with healthy food and water, and get moving as much as possible. Taking these physical steps will make you stronger and more able to take the mental steps necessary to overcome test anxiety.

Mental Steps for Beating Test Anxiety

Working on the mental side of test anxiety can be more challenging, but as with the physical side, there are clear steps you can take to overcome it. As mentioned earlier, test anxiety often stems from lack of preparation, so the obvious solution is to prepare for the test. Effective studying may be the most important weapon you have for beating test anxiety, but you can and should employ several other mental tools to combat fear.

First, boost your confidence by reminding yourself of past success—tests or projects that you aced. If you're putting as much effort into preparing for this test as you did for those, there's no reason you should expect to fail here. Work hard to prepare; then trust your preparation.

Second, surround yourself with encouraging people. It can be helpful to find a study group, but be sure that the people you're around will encourage a positive attitude. If you spend time with others who are anxious or cynical, this will only contribute to your own anxiety. Look for others who are motivated to study hard from a desire to succeed, not from a fear of failure.

Third, reward yourself. A test is physically and mentally tiring, even without anxiety, and it can be helpful to have something to look forward to. Plan an activity following the test, regardless of the outcome, such as going to a movie or getting ice cream.

When you are taking the test, if you find yourself beginning to feel anxious, remind yourself that you know the material. Visualize successfully completing the test. Then take a few deep, relaxing breaths and return to it. Work through the questions carefully but with confidence, knowing that you are capable of succeeding.

Developing a healthy mental approach to test taking will also aid in other areas of life. Test anxiety affects more than just the actual test—it can be damaging to your mental health and even contribute to depression. It's important to beat test anxiety before it becomes a problem for more than testing.

Study Strategy

Being prepared for the test is necessary to combat anxiety, but what does being prepared look like? You may study for hours on end and still not feel prepared. What you need is a strategy for test prep. The next few pages outline our recommended steps to help you plan out and conquer the challenge of preparation.

Step 1: Scope Out the Test

Learn everything you can about the format (multiple choice, essay, etc.) and what will be on the test. Gather any study materials, course outlines, or sample exams that may be available. Not only will this help you to prepare, but knowing what to expect can help to alleviate test anxiety.

Step 2: Map Out the Material

Look through the textbook or study guide and make note of how many chapters or sections it has. Then divide these over the time you have. For example, if a book has 15 chapters and you have five days to study, you need to cover three chapters each day. Even better, if you have the time, leave an extra day at the end for overall review after you have gone through the material in depth.

If time is limited, you may need to prioritize the material. Look through it and make note of which sections you think you already have a good grasp on, and which need review. While you are studying, skim quickly through the familiar sections and take more time on the challenging parts.

Write out your plan so you don't get lost as you go. Having a written plan also helps you feel more in control of the study, so anxiety is less likely to arise from feeling overwhelmed at the amount to cover.

Step 3: Gather Your Tools

Decide what study method works best for you. Do you prefer to highlight in the book as you study and then go back over the highlighted portions? Or do you type out notes of the important information? Or is it helpful to make flashcards that you can carry with you? Assemble the pens, index cards, highlighters, post-it notes, and any other materials you may need so you won't be distracted by getting up to find things while you study.

If you're having a hard time retaining the information or organizing your notes, experiment with different methods. For example, try color-coding by subject with colored pens, highlighters, or post-it notes. If you learn better by hearing, try recording yourself reading your notes so you can listen while in the car, working out, or simply sitting at your desk. Ask a friend to quiz you from your flashcards, or try teaching someone the material to solidify it in your mind.

Step 4: Create Your Environment

It's important to avoid distractions while you study. This includes both the obvious distractions like visitors and the subtle distractions like an uncomfortable chair (or a too-comfortable couch that makes you want to fall asleep). Set up the best study environment possible: good lighting and a comfortable work area. If background music helps you focus, you may want to turn it on, but otherwise keep the room quiet. If you are using a computer to take notes, be sure you don't have any other windows open, especially applications like social media, games, or anything else that could distract you. Silence your phone and turn off notifications. Be sure to keep water close by so you stay hydrated while you study (but avoid unhealthy drinks and snacks).

Also, take into account the best time of day to study. Are you freshest first thing in the morning? Try to set aside some time then to work through the material. Is your mind clearer in the afternoon or evening? Schedule your study session then. Another method is to study at the same time of day that you will take the test, so that your brain gets used to working on the material at that time and will be ready to focus at test time.

Step 5: Study!

Once you have done all the study preparation, it's time to settle into the actual studying. Sit down, take a few moments to settle your mind so you can focus, and begin to follow your study plan. Don't give in to distractions or let yourself procrastinate. This is your time to prepare so you'll be ready to fearlessly approach the test. Make the most of the time and stay focused.

Of course, you don't want to burn out. If you study too long you may find that you're not retaining the information very well. Take regular study breaks. For example, taking five minutes out of every hour to walk briskly, breathing deeply and swinging your arms, can help your mind stay fresh.

As you get to the end of each chapter or section, it's a good idea to do a quick review. Remind yourself of what you learned and work on any difficult parts. When you feel that you've mastered the material, move on to the next part. At the end of your study session, briefly skim through your notes again.

But while review is helpful, cramming last minute is NOT. If at all possible, work ahead so that you won't need to fit all your study into the last day. Cramming overloads your brain with more information than it can process and retain, and your tired mind may struggle to recall even previously learned information when it is overwhelmed with last-minute study. Also, the urgent nature of cramming and the stress placed on your brain contribute to anxiety. You'll be more likely to go to the test feeling unprepared and having trouble thinking clearly.

So don't cram, and don't stay up late before the test, even just to review your notes at a leisurely pace. Your brain needs rest more than it needs to go over the information again. In fact, plan to finish your studies by noon or early afternoon the day before the test. Give your brain the rest of the day to relax or focus on other things, and get a good night's sleep. Then you will be fresh for the test and better able to recall what you've studied.

Step 6: Take a Practice Test

Many courses offer sample tests, either online or in the study materials. This is an excellent resource to check whether you have mastered the material, as well as to prepare for the test format and environment.

Check the test format ahead of time: the number of questions, the type (multiple choice, free response, etc.), and the time limit. Then create a plan for working through them. For example, if you have 30 minutes to take a 60-question test, your limit is 30 seconds per question. Spend less time on the questions you know well so that you can take more time on the difficult ones.

If you have time to take several practice tests, take the first one open book, with no time limit. Work through the questions at your own pace and make sure you fully understand them. Gradually work up to taking a test under test conditions: sit at a desk with all study materials put away and set a timer. Pace yourself to make sure you finish the test with time to spare and go back to check your answers if you have time.

After each test, check your answers. On the questions you missed, be sure you understand why you missed them. Did you misread the question (tests can use tricky wording)? Did you forget the information? Or was it something you hadn't learned? Go back and study any shaky areas that the practice tests reveal.

Taking these tests not only helps with your grade, but also aids in combating test anxiety. If you're already used to the test conditions, you're less likely to worry about it, and working through tests until you're scoring well gives you a confidence boost. Go through the practice tests until you feel comfortable, and then you can go into the test knowing that you're ready for it.

Test Tips

On test day, you should be confident, knowing that you've prepared well and are ready to answer the questions. But aside from preparation, there are several test day strategies you can employ to maximize your performance.

First, as stated before, get a good night's sleep the night before the test (and for several nights before that, if possible). Go into the test with a fresh, alert mind rather than staying up late to study.

Try not to change too much about your normal routine on the day of the test. It's important to eat a nutritious breakfast, but if you normally don't eat breakfast at all, consider eating just a protein bar. If you're a coffee drinker, go ahead and have your normal coffee. Just make sure you time it so that the caffeine doesn't wear off right in the middle of your test. Avoid sugary beverages, and drink enough water to stay hydrated but not so much that you need a restroom break 10 minutes into the test. If your test isn't first thing in the morning, consider going for a walk or doing a light workout before the test to get your blood flowing.

Allow yourself enough time to get ready, and leave for the test with plenty of time to spare so you won't have the anxiety of scrambling to arrive in time. Another reason to be early is to select a good seat. It's helpful to sit away from doors and windows, which can be distracting. Find a good seat, get out your supplies, and settle your mind before the test begins.

When the test begins, start by going over the instructions carefully, even if you already know what to expect. Make sure you avoid any careless mistakes by following the directions.

Then begin working through the questions, pacing yourself as you've practiced. If you're not sure on an answer, don't spend too much time on it, and don't let it shake your confidence. Either skip it and come back later, or eliminate as many wrong answers as possible and guess among the remaining ones. Don't dwell on these questions as you continue—put them out of your mind and focus on what lies ahead.

Be sure to read all of the answer choices, even if you're sure the first one is the right answer. Sometimes you'll find a better one if you keep reading. But don't second-guess yourself if you do immediately know the answer. Your gut instinct is usually right. Don't let test anxiety rob you of the information you know.

If you have time at the end of the test (and if the test format allows), go back and review your answers. Be cautious about changing any, since your first instinct tends to be correct, but make sure you didn't misread any of the questions or accidentally mark the wrong answer choice. Look over any you skipped and make an educated guess.

At the end, leave the test feeling confident. You've done your best, so don't waste time worrying about your performance or wishing you could change anything. Instead, celebrate the successful completion of this test. And finally, use this test to learn how to deal with anxiety even better next time.

Review Video: Test Anxiety
Visit mometrix.com/academy and enter code: 100340

Important Qualification

Not all anxiety is created equal. If your test anxiety is causing major issues in your life beyond the classroom or testing center, or if you are experiencing troubling physical symptoms related to your anxiety, it may be a sign of a serious physiological or psychological condition. If this sounds like your situation, we strongly encourage you to seek professional help.

Online Resources

Due to our efforts to try to keep this book to a manageable length, we've created a link that will give you access to all of your online resources:

mometrix.com/resources719/ncetmb

It's Your Moment, Let's Celebrate It!

Share your story @mometrixtestpreparation